HIDDEN TREASURES

BRISTOL VOL I

Edited by Donna Samworth

First published in Great Britain in 2002 by
YOUNG WRITERS
Remus House,
Coltsfoot Drive,
Peterborough, PE2 9JX
Telephone (01733) 890066

All Rights Reserved

Copyright Contributors 2002

HB ISBN 0 75433 756 1
SB ISBN 0 75433 757 X

FOREWORD

This year, the Young Writers' Hidden Treasures competition proudly presents a showcase of the best poetic talent from over 72,000 up-and-coming writers nationwide.

Young Writers was established in 1991 and we are still successful, even in today's technologically-led world, in promoting and encouraging the reading and writing of poetry.

The thought, effort, imagination and hard work put into each poem impressed us all, and once again, the task of selecting poems was a difficult one, but nevertheless, an enjoyable experience.

We hope you are as pleased as we are with the final selection and that you and your family continue to be entertained with *Hidden Treasures Bristol Vol I* for many years to come.

Contents

	Rebecca Dimes	1
Elm Park Primary School		
	Suzanne Lester	1
	Bethany Smith	2
	Emma Chambers	2
	Tom Davis	3
	Louise Northam	4
	Hannah Webb	4
	Joseph Burton	5
	Daisy Teuton	6
Glenfrome Primary School		
	Nina McCondichie	6
	Jessica Clemmings	7
	Louie Campbell	8
	Hazel Phillips	8
	Sarah Macgregor	9
	Joseph Wicks-Humphreys	10
Henleaze Junior School		
	Theo Devine	10
	Rosamund Thomas	11
	Rosalind McClelland	11
	Catharine Hiley	12
	Ellen Cooper	12
	Anna Barham	13
	Zoe Jeffery	13
	Frances Stewart	14
	Ellen Cameron	14
	Hannah Cooper	15
	Tom George	15
	Jack Povey	16
	Jack Escritt	16
	Katy Dash	17
	Jenny Yard	17

Joanna Cordell	18
David Cordell	18
Billie Williams	19
Claire Sangster	20
Alice Ravenhill	20
Beth Evans	21
Luke Steven	22
Jennifer Sudworth	23
Rosie Brierley	24
Rebecca Bell	24
Jennifer Molton	25
Thomas Bowes	25
Jennifer Foster	26
Dastan Zorab	26
Mark Gollop	27
Sam Ardis	27
Niamh Stowe	28
Matthew Thomas	28
Alexandra Chlebko	29
Christian George	29
Imogen White	30
Natalie Ostréhan	30
William Payne	31
Robert Bryan-Smith	31
Scott Snell	32
Rosie Mussen	32
Emma Player	33
Charlotte Mason	33
Laura Boot	34
Sammy Paul	34
Thomas Hughes	35
Robert Maszuchin	35
Sylvie McDonough	36
Lucy Watson	36
Katie Andrews	37
Helen Battrick	37
Katie Rides	38
Dominic McInerney	38

Gemma Sandell	39
Thomas Pollitt	40
Nicole Harries	40
Ben McAndrew	41
Alexander Mayer	41
Julia Andrews	42
Glen Wood	42
Tom Campbell	43
Serena Lenz	43
Hope Gallie	44
Lauren Byrne	44
Emily Thompson	45
Henry Moody	45
Robbie White	46
Joseph Lovatt	47
Danielle Yeomans	47
Rebecca Steven	48
Jamie Hughes	48
Finan Rodinson	49
Becky Hughes	49
Emma Watson	50
Carla Ahmadi	50
Emily Adcock	50
Nicholas Adams	51
Stephanie Melarickas	51
Hattie Haynes	52
Louie Newlands	52
Stefan Pollitt	53
Emma White	53
Nicola Rees	54
Hazel Stenner	54
Max Molton	55

St Mary's CE Primary School

Rachel Drew	55
David Poole	56
Amber Crookes	57
Jennifer Jones	57

Sheryl Thompson	58
Rebecca Williams	58
Stephanie Thayer	59
Richard Organ	59
Heather Nicholls	60
Jenna Youell	60
Rachael Ware	61
Josh Gouge	61
Matthew Thomas	62
Mark Pearce	62
Ben Heath	62
Ryan Morgan	63
Jade Chisholm	63
Daniel Norris	63
Oliver Slade	64
Laura Cropley	64
Sophie Youell	65
Paul Timms	65
Timothy Higgs	66
Antony Jowett	66
Lauren Carr	67
Michael Radomski	67
Harry Drysdale-Groves	68
Amie Chinn	68
Lauren Saunders	69
Francesca Kelly	69
Ryan Brockwell	70
Elizabeth Seery	70
Laurence Murray	71
Verity Olivia Thorne	71
Sophie Youlden	72
Amy Greaves	72
Chloë Daniels	73
Claire Stirling	73
Marcus Skinner	74
Katie Lansdowne	74
Laura Prickett	75
David Pearman	75

Josh Matthews	76
Jade Flynn	76
Liam John	77
Hope Winton	77
Emily McKane	78
Toni York	78
Hazel Kirkham	78
Jim Pittaway	79
Liam Robert John	79
James Faulkner	80
Rachel Pellow	80
Bethany Gent	81
Charlotte Hall	81
Sophie Blackmore	81

St Teresa's School

Danielle Sealy	82
Bridie O'Neill	82
Luke Bowler	83
Patrick Maxwell	83
Caroline Voke	84
Maisie Milton-Newland	84
Ross Jones	85
Toni Stadon	86
Hannah Williams	86
Ben Summers	87
Ryan Cron	87
Julia Fox	88
Joseph Fitzgerald	88
Jade Clark	89
Joshua Williams	90
Reece Wynne	90
Rebecca Slater	91
Jordan Vailes	91
Ryan Jones	92
Quang Nguyen	92
Nathan Leaver	93
Stephen Dillon	94

Stockwood Green Primary School
- Madeleine Gould — 94
- Yat Man Chan & Charlotte Gallop — 95
- Lucy Seager & Emma Bowen — 95
- Casey Beardmore — 95
- Alice & Donna — 96

Summerhill Junior School
- Vicky Lovell — 96
- Martha Ellie Dennett — 97
- Alice Pople — 97
- Lucy Anning — 98
- Kerrii May Knighton — 98
- Nikita Patel — 99
- Lee Wilkins — 99
- Ellys Dickenson — 100
- Ashanti Walker — 101
- Jessica Roberts — 102
- Hannah Whittaker — 102
- Nicole Dicker — 103
- Hannah Richardson — 103
- Katie Morton — 104
- Mason Bowers — 104
- Jennifer Pretlove — 105
- Emily Church — 105
- Keagan Robinson — 106
- Caitlin O'Shea — 106
- Samantha Cox — 107
- Jack Jarrett — 107
- Georgia Mead — 108
- Rosie Gauge — 108
- Paige Nethercott — 109
- Rochelle Sheppard — 109
- Jade James — 110
- Ben Millard — 110
- Molly Winstanley — 111
- Becky Player — 111
- Nicola Gillam — 112

	Roxy Lawrence	112
	Kimberley Campbell	113
	Natalie Woods	113
	Bret Ryan Tizard	114

The Tynings School

	Mellisa Louise Szabunas	114
	Jack Andrews	115
	Reece Powell	115
	Hannah Durnell	116
	Katie Shipp	116
	Kate-Louise Fry	117
	Emma Hazlett	118
	Naomi Cassidy	118
	Alex Seymour	119
	Sam Elliott	120
	Ben Vincent	121
	Samantha Wood	122
	Faye Mason	122
	Connie Short	123
	Jade Morch	124
	James Cox	124
	Rebecca Jones	125
	Vicky Maggs	125
	Claudia Jacob	126
	Alex Gill	126

Wrington CE Primary School

	Simon Tourigny	127
	Simon Medd	127
	Mary Wratten	128
	Mathew Thorneywork	128
	Sophie Sleight	129
	Philippe Wilson	130
	Amber Hartley-Watts	130
	Joanna Kim Marshall	131
	Harvey Andrew Walters	132
	Rebecca Millard	132

Sophie Johnson	133
Hope Cadman	134
Matthew Beck	134
Amy Frampton	135
Louise Basey	135
Hannah Shirt	136
Jennifer Vowles	136
Andrew Lund	137
James Harris	138
Emma Gilling	138
Amy Vowles	139
Lucy Evans	140
Nicholas Higgs	140

The Poems

THE LION

A face like a fierce bear.
A mane like a pretty pink tutu.
Teeth like sharp daggers.
Eyes like huge raisins.
A leather moist nose.
Stalks prey in the undergrowth.

Rebecca Dimes (9)

THE SEA

The sea is a place where the seagulls meet,
People making sandcastles,
Children burying feet.

The sea is a place where people swim,
So don't drop rubbish in it,
Put it in the bin.

The sea is a place where they sell buckets and spades,
It's not like school,
Where they mark your work with good and bad grades.

The sea is a place where you can eat ice cream,
A lolly too,
If you're lucky.

The sea is a place where you can dip your toes,
It's lots of fun,
Have a good time playing in the sun,
Smell that salt spray with your nose!

Suzanne Lester (9)
Elm Park Primary School

I'M ALWAYS GETTING INTO TROUBLE

I'm always getting into trouble,
My mummy says so too,
But in some ways I am loveable,
Only when I'm on my loo.

I'm always getting into trouble,
I always get told off,
I say I hate it very much,
The teacher starts to cough.

I'm always getting into trouble,
You see I don't like it all,
It's like the time when I broke my bed in the night,
I fell right to the floor.

I just want to say sorry,
For all the bad things I have done,
So listen to me carefully,
I'm sorry everyone.

Bethany Smith (9)
Elm Park Primary School

MERMAID LIFE

Under sea,
Where fish leap,
Treasure-laden on the bed,
That's where the mermaids sleep.

Sharks dive,
As if alive,
Men are searching for the treasure,
That's where the mermaids play.

Rocks slide,
Volcanoes burst,
Lava flows,
That's the Mermaid Adventure Park.

Emma Chambers (9)
Elm Park Primary School

THE SCHOOL IDIOT

As I walked into school for another boring day
Because at nine o'clock chaos starts
As the school idiot arrives

As he walks through the gate and crashes into the tree
He walks over and starts to talk to me

It's a whole lot of blabber
Yet I still listen
As the school bell rings
My hope has not risen

As we walk into class
The idiot banging his head
I sit down and write
Wishing I was in bed

At the end of the day when I finally escape school
I walk home and get into bed
My heart full of dread for tomorrow's
Another day to await the school idiot.

Tom Davis (9)
Elm Park Primary School

TEACHER'S PET

My teacher, Miss Mongree,
Has a pet and it is me.
I help her with her work and chores,
She replies with 'Great' or 'Sure.'

My friends should mind their own business, I can choose,
They call me 'teacher's pet' or 'goody-two-shoes'.
They really do upset me,
So I tell my best friend, Miss Mongree.

I will always stick with her,
I'm like a cat as I purr.
I don't care what anyone thinks of me,
Because I have my teacher, Miss Mongree.

Louise Northam (10)
Elm Park Primary School

NOISES IN THE NIGHT

When you're in your snugly bed
You never know what might happen,
There might be ghosts or monsters lurking
Or noises in the night.

It might be something in your bedroom
Or something outside,
It might be right now in your bed
Or just noises in the night.

It might go creeping up on you
To scare you out of town,
It might be standing by the door
Or noises in the night.

It may just be shadows
Of ghosts and monsters too,
Look! Who's that?
'Mum?'

Hannah Webb (10)
Elm Park Primary School

MESSY ROOM

My room is a mess
I can't help it
It just seems to be like that
I clean it and clean it,
But still it's a tip
Stuff just falls and is never picked up
Lego pieces are left but Mum doesn't care
Unlike me
It really does my head in,
But then on the Tuesday just gone
No mess!

Till under the bed I had a peep
Just before I went to sleep
I saw Lego bits and toys galore
And that's why my room is clean no more.

Joseph Burton (9)
Elm Park Primary School

STORM

The wind howls like a hungry wolf
Flying through the trees
I cover my ears to block the sound,
But I don't succeed

Lightning flashes
And thunder rumbles
Like my hungry stomach
I need food desperately

Suddenly everything is quiet
The storm dies down
I fall peacefully asleep
As a rainbow forms.

Daisy Teuton (10)
Elm Park Primary School

MY WIND

On top of my mountain, my wind is strong,
Next to my sea, my wind calms me,
In the sky I have never been,
The wind up there I've never felt nor seen.
Never will I hope,
Down here I should happily stay,
With my mountain,
My sea
And best of all,
My wind.

Nina McCondichie (8)
Glenfrome Primary School

BEWARE

He's big and he's hairy,
He's probably scary.
You better watch out,
There is a monster about.
His eyes are green,
He'll smash your house to smithereens.
You better watch out, there's a monster about.
Of all the monsters in the country,
This one had to land here in Muck Humfy.
He's slimy and smelly,
Smellier than your dad's wellies.
So you better watch out,
There's a monster about.
I don't like to describe this horrible creature,
That's because he's worse than my teacher.
So you better watch out,
There's a monster about.
I can't believe my mum's making such a fuss,
I only saw it when I got off the bus.
My sister keeps screaming,
But only when she's dreaming.
My brother thinks it's funny,
But my dad is really worried.
You better watch out,
There's a monster about.

Jessica Clemmings (9)
Glenfrome Primary School

MAGICAL CHRISTMAS

I ran into the living room with my eyes closed.
The smell was Christmassy, fresh, woody.
I suddenly opened my eyes,
An enormous Christmas tree rose from the floor,
Its feet planted firmly in a rusty bucket.

Red, blue and yellow twinkling brightly,
Like sun shining on water.
Linked together with green ribbon,
I could barely see them,
A spider's web of flickering magic.

Mysterious boxes wrapped up with sparkling paper,
Which lit up the room.
Glistening globes dangling from the spiky fingers,
Chocolate and toffee sticks tempting me
And right at the top, a beaming star.

Louie Campbell (8)
Glenfrome Primary School

IF YOU WERE A DOG . . .

If you were a dog you would:
Dream of bones all day,
Wish to go for walkies,
Dig holes in flower beds,
Scratch the door until it nearly breaks,
Chew your lead to shreds,
Sleep and then wake everyone in the morning,
Eat your food and lap your water,
Run about like mad,

Play fetch with your owner,
Lick your owner 'til they're soggy,
Jump up at toddlers and make them cry,
Rip pages out of books
And eventually get so tired you fall asleep
And dream of bones
And going for walkies
And digging holes in flower beds and . . .

Hazel Phillips (10)
Glenfrome Primary School

WHAT ADULTS DO

What adults do,
Adults stand and talk all day,
Adults sit and talk all day,
They talk about themselves,
They talk about others,
They talk about kids,
Holidays, ships, cars, schools,
They talk about everything,
They talk about money,
Jobs, transport, friends, books,
They talk about everything,
Adults talk about animals,
They talk about cats,
They talk about everything
And bore me to death.

Sarah Macgregor (9)
Glenfrome Primary School

THE LIFE SHOP

Once there lived a life shop,
My favourite place to go.
They had all sorts of lives,
Good ones, bad ones, even sad ones.

But there was one life sitting on the top shelf,
Full of sadness, anger, vengeance
And it just sat there,
But this life was my life.

It just sat there shaking on the shelf,
With its anger and sadness.
All the others were relaxing in their good,
Wealthy lives without a bother or care.

Even till this day nobody has bought my life.

Joseph Wicks-Humphreys (9)
Glenfrome Primary School

THE GOLDEN HARBOUR

I sailed across the sea
Day and night
Past the rocks and distant lands
Storms and tidal waves
Whipped the ship
At last I came to the golden harbour
Where the booty lies
Aarrghh! I found the blinking treasure
Shivering sharks, I'm rich!

Theo Devine (9)
Henleaze Junior School

QUIDDITCH

Harry dives and flies
As the golden snitch hides.
Black bludgers race across the sky,
Darting colours of red, yellow, green and blue.

Fading cheers from the crowd,
A huge sign saying, 'Go on Harry, that's out lad'.
The glaze of gold passes by,
Harry sees his chance and dives!

Crack of thunder,
Lightning struck,
It fell into his hands,
He couldn't believe his luck.

Harry held the snitch with shaking hands,
He'd won the match!
The team came down
And Harry was famous all over town!

Rosamund Thomas (9)
Henleaze Junior School

THE BEACH

Along the sandy banks of the sparkling sea,
Crawling crabs clamber over the rocks,
People bathe in the brightness of the blazing sun,
Waves and water are whipped by the wind,
Sandy sandwiches, sandy bananas, sandy *everything*.

The beach!

Rosalind McClelland (9)
Henleaze Junior School

THERE WAS AN OLD WOMAN WHO LIVED IN A SHOE

There was an old woman who lived in a shoe,
Had so many children she didn't know what to do,
To give them their broth without any bread?
To not read them a story when they went to bed?
This old woman who lived in a shoe,
Had so many children but knew what to do.
To make them their breakfast; porridge and toast,
To send them outside while making the roast.
To let them eat slowly or just as they pleased,
To answer them politely when they had just sneezed.
To let them hang round her and pester all day,
Or go up to the shoelace to swing or to play.
To make them their favourite meal for tea,
The children all thought of one thing which was 'me'.
To read them a story of Three Little Pigs
And how they all danced in tiny grey wigs.
To tuck them up tightly and kiss them goodnight,
To close up the curtains and switch off the light.
So this is the end of the old woman's day,
To look after the children; for them she will pray:
'God bless my dear children in all that they do,
God bless my dear children that live in my shoe.'

Catharine Hiley (11)
Henleaze Junior School

SPOOKS

In a dark, dark house lived a little mouse,
All the things I think are there, just lurking on the stair.
Creeping along to the bedroom to find me there,
Every shadow I see, I think to myself, it's only me.

Ellen Cooper (7)
Henleaze Junior School

A SHOOTING STAR

There's a star shooting in the sky,
Close to the moon, so high, so high,
Here come the scientists, they're going to see
How this star could affect you and me.
Oh look, this star is coming close!
This gives us a chance to see a space ghost.
This star's a special one, bright, shining, new,
Is this the star that will make my dreams come true?
I will make this star stay up in the sky,
Oh no, the star is about to die,
But maybe there's another star giving birth,
I think this is the best star
On the Earth!

Anna Barham (9)
Henleaze Junior School

THE THREE BEARS

The three bears went out for a walk,
But only really to have a talk!
They counted themselves a 1, 2, 3,
Then they all shouted 'Yippee!'
When they all strolled back into their house,
There was nothing moving, not even a mouse
When all three of them had walked up the stairs,
Over in the corner, in the chairs,
Sat one little madam who was asleep!
One of the bears let out a loud scream,
Then the girl woke up with a big beam!
She ran as quickly as she could,
Far away into the woods!

Zoe Jeffery (11)
Henleaze Junior School

The Ghost Hunter

I'm going on a trip today
With my sister, my mum and my dad,
Mum said 'We are going to a castle'
I'm really not too glad.
Today we got a card
With a graveyard on it.
Mum pointed out the tombstones,
One had a skull and crossbones.
Dad said we were going to a place that
Had a very, very old legend . . .
That at 6 and 7 every night,
A ghost hunter would
Give you a *fright!*

Frances Stewart (8)
Henleaze Junior School

You'll Be Spooked

Last night I heard a thud,
I was in the graveyard,
I said to myself 'There's somebody there!
There's somebody haunted, as haunted as can be!
There's creaking and cracking and blood dripping from the steeple.'

I saw the trees wailing in the wind,
I saw the door flapping,
I saw the curtain torn and flapping with the wind.
I saw a deathly shape,
Big and ghostly,
I think I'd better run!

Ellen Cameron (8)
Henleaze Junior School

WHAT IS A SUBJECT?

What is a subject?
That's what I want to know.
Is it like a TV
Or more like a big toe?

If I came across a subject,
One day wandering in the park,
How am I to know it's a subject
And not a misplaced shark?

Is a subject round and fat
Or is it short or tall?
Is a subject really big
Or is it really small?

Are subjects a real mystery
Or am I just a fool?
If you really want to know the truth,
I don't know at all.

Hannah Cooper (11)
Henleaze Junior School

THE ZOMBIE SIGHT

At midnight the zombies rise,
Each night they haunt another house,
But when I go there, there's not a sound about,
But once I went at midnight
And the zombies haunted me.
So now I'm a zombie.

Tom George (7)
Henleaze Junior School

WHAT CAN WE DO TODAY?

What can we do today
To keep the playground tidy and neat?
Come along, surprise me,
No rubbish I wish to meet!

Pick up all the crisp packets,
That is what we can do today,
Pick up all the candy wrappers,
From the park when we go to play.

Put the rubbish out in the recycle bin,
To keep our environment clean,
All of the old newspapers, bottles and tins,
My family are a dedicated team.

Put all of the toys in the toy box,
Put my slippers under the bed,
That is what we can do today,
To keep the world tidy instead!

Jack Povey (9)
Henleaze Junior School

GHOST HUNTER

He darts through the night,
He squeezes through the alleyway as tight as tight,
For catching ghosts is his mission,
He puts them in a glass prison,
For his pet snake, a very good treat,
Something he likes to eat and eat,
But in the morning, you can't see
The way he keeps the world in harmony.

Jack Escritt (8)
Henleaze Junior School

ALADDIN

Aladdin, Aladdin,
A lad in a jar.
Caught there and put there,
By wicked Jafar.

We need a genie,
To let our lad out.
If you should see one,
Give me a shout.

Behind you! Behind you!
A boo and a hiss.
What a lad needs
Is a princess's kiss.

You can decide
The end of our tale.
Will our Aladdin
Succeed or just . . . *stay in the jar!*

Katy Dash (10)
Henleaze Junior School

I KNOW A PERSON . . .

I know a person
Who walks the haunted tower,
Her name is Anne Boleyn,
Who comes out at the hour,
She comes out at the hour,
Bang on midnight,
She comes to haunt the tower,
As long as it's not light.

Jenny Yard (7)
Henleaze Junior School

THE SNOWDROP

The snowdrop's little head is white,
The marigold is *huge* compared to her height.

Whenever she falls fast asleep,
The rose awakens her and she starts to weep.

Even though she is full of peace,
The snowdrop releases her petals.

Even though her leaves do droop,
The ivy is at his worst with his twisty loops.

The snowdrop's birth in freezing cold February,
Lasts for 3 or 4 months before her leaves die.

The snowdrop shivered and said with a sneeze,
'This would be better if I rest my leaves!'

And then the other flowers were told,
The snowdrop cried because she was cold.

So never forget the snowdrop's call,
'Lend me your gloves, your scarf and your shawl!'

Joanna Cordell (9)
Henleaze Junior School

WHEN I WENT DIVING

When I went diving in the sea
I met a shark who said to me
'Of all the men that I have met
You look the tastiest morsel yet

Your chewy fingers, your lardy toes
Your squishy eyeballs, your savoury nose
I will squash you, you little squirt
Mash you up with mud and dirt'

I said I wouldn't stand for that
He advanced one foot and I squashed him flat
He went off crying to his mum
And round the corner she did come

Her huge gilled head, her back a bump
A massive hill of a rump
Her eyes turned red, her mouth grew wider
And down I went, quite deep inside 'er.

David Cordell (11)
Henleaze Junior School

MY FRIEND THE GHOUL

I know a person
His name is Leigh
He lives in a haunted house
As spooky as can be

He lies at school about himself,
But when he is at the haunted house
He is actually a vampire

His broom is under the staircase
His hat is in the cellar
His robe is in his school bag
And his sister is called Bella

He closes his mouth all day at school,
But under those lips is a ghoul

He has vampire teeth under that bad lip
That no one wants to see
When he's at school
He really frightens me.

Billie Williams (8)
Henleaze Junior School

THE MARTIAN

A big round disk flew out of the sky,
It stopped and hovered then something said hi.
A Martian that was green and white,
Came out of the spaceship in a flash of light.
He was wearing a pair of polka dot shorts
And his face was covered in spots and warts.
He gave an old lady some lovely flowers,
But they gave the lady some magic powers.
So she sent the Martian back to his disk,
Then the Martian began to whisk,
A beautiful cake that was chocolate in flavour
And this was just for a little favour.

Soon after that the Martian said bye,
But accidentally poked himself in the eye,
So we helped him to bandage it up
And then we gave him a little cup
Of soup and carrots and lots of green things.
Then he began to flap his wings
And sent himself to his spaceship,
Just for fun he did a backwards flip,
Then he went flying up into the sky,
Whilst we all shouted, 'Bye-bye!'

Claire Sangster (10)
Henleaze Junior School

CHANGING CLOUDS

Storm clouds race across the sky
Setting sail for Arab's Dubai
A state of rich from gas and oil
They sail their ships, above the waves they fall.

Still in rage they see their end
Now happy signals homely send
The storm clouds change from black to white
As their destination draws in to sight.

Alice Ravenhill (9)
Henleaze Junior School

SLEEPING BEAUTY PARODY

Once there was a princess fair,
Who bought dozens of pairs of pink underwear,
But then one day a lady came,
A servant girl or something the same,
She came to teach the young princess,
How to sew to make a dress,
She brought only one needle,
The princess put one finger on the end, it began to bleed,
So she shouted 'Oh tweedle.'
She then fell asleep waiting for a soppy kiss,
Only a prince could compete with this.
So there she lay for many years,
Her parents wept some bitter tears,
Until one day Prince Albert came,
His fashion sense was really lame,
He came to kiss her,
Though no one really missed her,
But there came a scream from the princess's mouth,
'Get off you brute,
I was expecting someone a bit more cute.'
So the princess never married him,
She would have rather lost a limb.

Beth Evans (10)
Henleaze Junior School

OH PUFFERFISH

Oh Zebedee,
My pufferfish,
How sharp your spikes are today.
Oh Zebedee,
My pufferfish,
Would you like to come out to play?
Oh Bently,
My lionfish,
How stripy your scales have become.
Oh Bently,
My lionfish,
How I love to stroke your soft tum.
Oh Caroline,
My jellyfish,
I do admire your poisonous sting.
Oh Caroline,
My jellyfish,
Oh you make my heart just ring.
Oh Linet,
My parrotfish,
How I adore your smooth, small beak.
Oh Linet,
My parrotfish,
Oh I am sorry that your tank must leak.
How I did adore my beautiful fish,
They really did make a wonderful dish!

Luke Steven (10)
Henleaze Junior School

PLEASE MR WORDLEY

Please Mr Wordley,
This boy Ben McB,
Keeps stealing all my pencils, Sir,
Will you please help me?

Well, let's see what I can do now,
Let me see . . . I know!
Go and sit next to Rosebud, there,
The one with the purple bow!

Please Mr Wordley,
This boy Kai-no Jack
Keeps using all my gel pens Sir,
He's getting on my back!

Shove your pen case down the toilet,
Put it in your drawer,
Now please don't ask me any questions,
My brain is getting sore!

Please Mr Wordley,
This girl Rachel A,
Keeps calling me rude names Sir,
There's the bell! Bye! Hey!

At last! At last!
The bell has gone, hooray!
At last! At last!
See you another day!

Jennifer Sudworth (8)
Henleaze Junior School

THE HAUNTED HOUSE

Creep through the hallway,
Go down the stairs,
Go through the porch way
And open the door,
Go down the street
And open the door of the haunted house,
Go through the porch way of the haunted house,
Go up the stairs,
Lean against the wall,
The wall moves,
I heard a scream, 'aarrghh,'
Then I see a vampire coming towards me,
I push the wall,
Run to the door and open it,
Run down the stairs,
Open the door of the haunted house
And home I go!

Rosie Brierley (7)
Henleaze Junior School

MY GRANDFATHER'S HAUNTED ROOM

My grandfather has a clock,
Tick-tock, tick-tock,
That sometimes grows hands and legs,
Tick-tock, tick-tock,
And when it grows hands and legs,
Tick-tock, tick-tock,
Everything else starts to move,
Tick-tock, tick-tock.

Rebecca Bell (8)
Henleaze Junior School

THE FLYING SENSATION

When I took off in quite a hurry,
The flying sensation I'll never forget.
The wind through my face
And the joy in my heart,
I wish we could never fly far apart.

Flying through the towering clouds,
It's like swimming through the sea,
The big, blue, breezy sky,
The burning red-hot sun,
Now I'm getting homesick,
I want my mum!

I bet you wish you were up here now,
Having loads of fun,
Wait!
What's that ahead of me?
Just round a couple of bends,
Way hey!
You won't believe it, it's all of my best, best friends.

Jennifer Molton (9)
Henleaze Junior School

LAZY!

I'm as lazy as a daisy blowing in the wind,
The dandelions parachute with the seeds on the end,
Letting the parachute do all the work for them,
Like slaves in the blowing wind.

Thomas Bowes (8)
Henleaze Junior School

The Haunted Caravan

The thing that worries my friend and I
Is the caravan that lies right outside.

I know it's haunted because
Each night it moans and groans.

I think it's full of ghosts and ghouls,
Because each night I hear their ghastly calls.

Whoo! Whoo! It goes each night,
That's what freaks me out all right.

The thing that worries my friend and I
Is the caravan that lies right outside.

Jennifer Foster (7)
Henleaze Junior School

Ghost Island

At Ghost Island there's a lot of ghosts,
Some with curly hair and faces like a pear.
Some sell pepperoni, some sell cheese and onion crisps,
Even though they don't like it, they still sell chips.

Some have curly moustaches,
Some go on the wooden thing
And some have a big chin.

Some have an identical twin,
Some have their head chopped off
And some have dogs that go woof woof.

Dastan Zorab (7)
Henleaze Junior School

THE STORM

The lightning fills up the sky
like bursts of lava from a volcano.

The thunder strikes, knocking trees down
like lots of skittles at the bowling alley.

Rain falls hard and hits the ground,
making puddles that grow bigger and bigger.

The wind pushes people, tossing them around,
they scream for help as they hurry home.

Inside their homes, the people draw their curtains
and light their fires, but they can still hear the crash of thunder,
the whistling wind and the continuous pitter-patter of the rain
on the windows as it races to the ground.

Mark Gollop (8)
Henleaze Junior School

DRAGON!

Dragon flying through the muttering wind,
He sees the crunching, crinkling leaves blowing through the air.
He flies through a misty breeze,
Feeling the rough wind slow him down
Like a bird out of breath.
There is nothing but a bed full of dust.
His wings slowing down because of the freezing hailstones.
He finds his cave, full of fog
And echoes of dogs.
His big eyes dance around
As they catch a burning flame,
Lulling him to sleep.

Sam Ardis (8)
Henleaze Junior School

GREEN FINGERS

I went into a room one day,
Full of spider webs it was.
And then I saw a bed,
It was up against the wall.

It was covered in dust
And wet it was.
I searched it more and more,
I did
Until I saw!

A pair of green fingers,
I was scared to death I was,
And I never went back there again.

Niamh Stowe (7)
Henleaze Junior School

DARK!

When you're walking
Near the park,
Are you afraid of the dark?

At the bottom of the sea,
Nobody has gone as deep as me.

In my bedroom at night,
I never get a big fright!

When you're walking
Near the park,
Are you afraid of the dark?

Matthew Thomas (7)
Henleaze Junior School

SPRINGTIME

April showers
And a soft
Breeze blows.
Lilies on a pond
Starting to grow.
Light nights
with warmer weather.
Bluebells
Start to
Show.
Leaves appearing
On the trees.
Flowers budding, and
Along comes
A bee.
Daffodils, golden yellow
And grass
So bright green.
Lambs being born
In the meadow
With bunnies hopping to and fro.

Alexandra Chlebko (8)
Henleaze Junior School

MY UNUSUAL SNAKE

Its tongue is like a dinner fork
Its scales are like dragon's skin
Its eyes are like black beads
If you try its poison you will not live.

Christian George (10)
Henleaze Junior School

THE SUMMER CAT

Once upon a summertime,
When all the leaves were green,
A little girl stroked the cat,
So not to be seen.

Her fingers laughed as they ran about,
Just like some fish in a blur,
They went from top to tail,
Through silky charcoal fur.

The cat miaowed and stretched her legs,
She sprang onto her lap,
Purring softly,
Snuggling down,
She had a little nap.

Waking up with daggers drawn,
Stretching in her mournful way,
She boldly took steps away from the girl,
Into the end of the day.

Imogen White (8)
Henleaze Junior School

THE SONG

The song of the south which sings high and low
The smell of a daffodil dancing in the snow
The laugh of a woman singing very high
The tap of a tap dancer tapping very fast
The eyelash from the eye which brings a silent tear
So listen to me, this might sound weird
Because of this magical poem I did.

Natalie Ostréhan (9)
Henleaze Junior School

THE BLACK-CAPED MAN

The Earth was shaking,
The birds were weeping,
The clouds were getting darker,
Thunder was beginning to strike,
The black-caped man appeared.

He swung his cape over his shoulder and growled,
The Earth shook,
Then he took his cape from his back,
Finally his cape flew into the night.

The night was getting more bright,
The gate creaked
And the black bars shivered,
A raven appeared with a letter,
It whispered . . .
Morning spell.

William Payne (9)
Henleaze Junior School

SUNSET

Look at it! It's coming to play,
It looks like a red bun burning away.

Look at the colours blossoming in the air,
It looks like a long strip of hair.

Look at the horizon, it goes on forever,
It never changes whatever the weather.

The sun is fading away, slipping into Heaven's bay,
It is flying in the air like a dragon in its lair.

Robert Bryan-Smith (8)
Henleaze Junior School

THE VILLAGE DUMP

The village had a dark sky,
As dark and as clear as a pair of brand new shoes
And nearby was the dump.
Ivy covered all the pieces of bottles and wood.
As you enter in the dark spooky cave,
Walls of bottles and glass shone in the firelight.
Wrappers and string stuck to the mud on the ceiling.
A chimney made from old paint tins clanked in the corner.
In the corner was a big pile of sharp bottles.
Fire blazing, like steam coming out of a volcano.
On the ground was a pair of old, smelly socks.
A pile of slippery, slimy, smelly mud carpeted the floor.
An ugly ogre stood in the corner,
Green with huge staring eyes.
He was pointing at the chimney made of clanky tins.
Magazines, hats, clothes and toys were scattered all over the floor.
It looked like a child's room.

Scott Snell (8)
Henleaze Junior School

MY RAT

As I stroke her welcoming fur,
I wonder how anyone could consider this beautiful creature as vermin.
She looks at me,
Her whiskers twitch in an alert way.
A bush taps against the window and her ears prick up suddenly.
Her fur is as soft as silk,
Her eyes like stars in a dark pool.
She is as delicate as a flower,
My rat.

Rosie Mussen (9)
Henleaze Junior School

THE SPOOKY GARDEN AND THE HAUNTED HOUSE

My garden isn't normal, neither is my house,
My garden is spooky, frightening too,
Everyone runs away when it grows dark in my garden.

Now come inside my house and look around,
There are bats and rats and cats all over the floor
And cobwebs on the door.
Come upstairs into my room and look about,
Can you see my cats eating rats?

A ghost haunts my garden,
A monster haunts my house,
Everyone runs away when it grows dark in my house.

All the cats eat rats,
All the cobwebs are on the door,
Now come up into the attic,
Where the cobwebs and bats live,
Oh yes a vampire haunts my attic,
Ahhh!
There's a spider!

Emma Player (8)
Henleaze Junior School

THE HORSE

The horse is as black as the night
It runs like the wind
Its soft fur, silky and smooth
Its name is Lightning
It jumps over the fence
Then is *gone.*

Charlotte Mason (9)
Henleaze Junior School

THE WITCH

The witch sneaks around at night
She gives people an awful fright
She has a cat that's black and white
And he is a terrible sight

The moon is bright
That's full of light
The witch can be seen at night
Riding her broomstick cackling with delight

She met a man
Who drove in a van,
Who had a tan,
Who was called Stan,
They fell in love and got wed
They're still together, so it's said.

Laura Boot (8)
Henleaze Junior School

THE FOUR DRAGONS
(This poem is dedicated in memory of Auntie Doris who would have loved to hear it)

The winter dragon ices up the lakes,
The winter dragon, warm weather he takes.
The spring dragon makes flowers dance,
The spring dragon makes the lambs prance.
The summer dragon makes the sun shine bright,
The summer dragon makes long days a delight.
The autumn dragon makes the leaves fall,
The autumn dragon gives conkers to all!

Sammy Paul (8)
Henleaze Junior School

MY FIELD AT CHRISTMAS TIME

I love my field at Christmas time
It's lovely and white
Like a sheet of paper
And all the houses look like snow

I love my field at Christmas time
I love riding my white pony called Snowy
And I can see the sky as white as the ground
I ride round with my brother and sister until I have to stop

And in the night, white owls come out and play
And swoop like snowflakes
And the trees are like white laces
And bushes like big lumps of snow.

Thomas Hughes (9)
Henleaze Junior School

WHITE NIGHT

The floor white with icicles
Laces my path.
The snowflakes fill my footsteps,
Covering my tracks.
I walk through the blanketed town,
The frosty snow hugs the river.
Snow glides from the windows,
Lights turn off.
The snowflakes jump up and down,
Tickling my shoes.
Rats scurry to the sewer for shelter,
Silhouetted against the icy glare.
The floor white with icicles blocks my path.

Robert Maszuchin (8)
Henleaze Junior School

The Garden

I opened the rusty gate
And what a sight met me!
Tulips grew in clumps on the flower bed,
On a little bridge going over the top of the stream
A few children were playing 'Pooh Sticks'.
A nearby gardener was bending over a little folly muttering
'Now where shall I put this primrose?'
I rolled over in my sleep and then awoke,
I was surprised it had been a dream.
It had seemed so real,
As real as a book!

The next night I went to sleep and found my garden again
And I noticed a sundial made completely out of marble.
A nearby bunch of daffodils danced in the wind.
A small amount of ivy swirled around a beautifully-crafted birdbath.
Birds seemed happy to eat food,
A wooden birdbath carved in the shape of a house rested in the shade.
I left my garden,
Never to see it again.

Sylvie McDonough (9)
Henleaze Junior School

The Koala

His knife-like claws grip the firm eucalyptus bark,
His rubbery nose strokes the smooth tree,
His soft, silky ears twitch in the gentle breeze
And his smoky-coloured paws brush the damp eucalyptus.
He curls up on the comfortable branch
For another eighteen hours' peaceful sleep.

Lucy Watson (11)
Henleaze Junior School

THE FOX

Darkness falls
Sleek and sly
Creeping through the misty night
Searching among the morsel delicacies
Finding; nothing
Seeing; nothing
Smelling; nothing
Getting slimmer and smaller each day
Soon the inky blackness will swallow him up
The black quilt embroidered with stars clears
Sunlight arrives
Crouching in a vent
Waiting, hoping, almost praying that someone would come by
And drop food or money
Another day gone, no hope, no food, no nothing
Time to go scavenging again
Darkness falls . . .

Katie Andrews (10)
Henleaze Junior School

THE CAT

The cat is as black as soot,
His tail swishes in the moonlight
And his paws pad on the soft undergrowth.
When he hears a noise his ears prick up,
He is as quiet as a mouse,
Nobody ever hears him.
His emerald eyes flicker like candles dancing in the breeze,
His nose twitches as he picks up a scent,
He is the cat of the night.

Helen Battrick (9)
Henleaze Junior School

PUSSY CAT

It's small at first
And then it grows
Be it a beauty or a drag
They're either black or ginger etc
The colours can go to blue and purple
Just wait and see
It purrs and miaows
All day and night
It growls at the other cats
In its pride
And scratches and whines
At the door
To escape from the indoor prison
When it's out
It's an outdoor prison
And wants to go in,
But it doesn't
So the poor little cat
Has nowhere to go
Just Hell or Heaven
Where will it go?

Katie Rides (11)
Henleaze Junior School

ONCE UPON A STARRY NIGHT

Once upon a starry night,
Flying freely, a wondrous flight,
Saw a shooting star, a glamorous sight,
Once upon a starry night.

Once upon a starry night,
I saw an alien, gave me a fright.
It came over to me, tried to bite,
Once upon a starry night.

Once upon a starry night,
I saw some stars in the shape of a kite.
Not many colours, just yellow and white,
Once upon a starry night.

Dominic McInerney (10)
Henleaze Junior School

CINDERELLA

People think they know the story well,
When the fairy godmother comes and casts a spell,
But this is different, wait and see,
It really isn't what it seems to be.

So this is how it all started,
There was the three sisters who were very kind-hearted,
Then there was evil but pretty Cinderella,
Not to forget her stepmother, Bella.

One day an important letter came,
But only for Cinderella, what a shame!
She opened it and guess what she saw?
An invite from the prince to his royal ball.

She looked rather pleased and said with a cackle,
'What to wear will be something to tackle.'
And so she came to the ball that night,
She looked so pretty, she was a lovely sight.

They danced a little, then the prince said in an angry tone,
'You'll never have any of my throne!'
That's right, he said he wouldn't marry Cinderella,
Instead he said he wanted to marry Bella.

Then to Cinderella's shock,
In came Bella in her lovely frock . . .

Gemma Sandell (10)
Henleaze Junior School

THE NIGHT

Through the trees, the somewhat ominous looking
night-time clouds are high up luminous faces,
smiling their evil smiles, glaring their heinous glares.
The rain-drenched branches of the night trees are
outstretched sweaty hands
trying desperately to seize a target that is by a
fraction, out of its terrible grasping range.
The trees themselves, powering machines,
overwhelmingly robust,
but yet, cannot with all their force, move a whisker
upon their own accord.
The night itself is a colossal developing, coal-black,
velvety-black mouth,
that swallows up half the world and all it can
elsewhere consume, each half day.
Swirling, swirling, ever closer;
the night is here for all to know.

Thomas Pollitt (11)
Henleaze Junior School

THE POLICEMAN

There was a policeman called Paul
Who was a little bit small
He liked to play football
And not to fight crime,
But did not do much at any time

He liked to eat pizza
And all the stuff like that,
But although he had to go to work
He always looked after Jasper, his cat.

Nicole Harries (9)
Henleaze Junior School

MY DAD GOT PECKED BY A DUCK

It was a down and dismal day
And the sky was grey,
The rain was dripping down
And everyone had a frown,
But then,
Dad got pecked by a duck
And Mum just said it was luck,
Then I just said it was a duck
And Dad got it for luck.
But then Dad slipped down the river
And started to quiver,
Then we all started to laugh
And Dad said 'You're all daft.'
We all went home chuckling
And chuckling.

Ben McAndrew (9)
Henleaze Junior School

RAIN

I love rain
Tipper-tappering on my window
Raindrops like silver hearts
Filling ponds

Rain has a touch of love

A sprinkling from God's hands
Across the world.

Alexander Mayer (8)
Henleaze Junior School

I FELL IN THE POND

We all grumbled, the sky was dull
We were bored, there was nothing to do
We were all going home to bed till
I fell
In
The
Pond
I screamed, I shouted, I grumbled, I giggled
Hattie was laughing, hooray, well done
Dad tried to pull me out (he said I weighed a ton)
We went back home, I had some cream
Yum! Yum!

The next day we went out and about
We went to the sea, just Mum and me
I had a cup of coffee and some tea
Nothing exciting happened that day
Until we came home, hip hip hooray!

Julia Andrews (9)
Henleaze Junior School

MYSTERY

I climbed out of bed
And went down the unstable stairs,
Through the creaky door,
Down the stony path,
Past the snake's skull jammed on the gatepost,
Into the whispering forest.
Past the sign: *Danger*,
Past the wolf with flesh-ripping jaws.
Never to return!

Glen Wood (8)
Henleaze Junior School

SEA VOICES

Have you heard the sea voices,
Whispering like the wind?
The voices echo in the night,
The voices rumble in the day,
Oh! Have you heard the sea voices?

Have you heard the sea voices,
Shimmering like the golden sand?
The voices echo in the night,
The voices rumble in the day,
Oh! Have you heard the sea voices?

Have you heard the sea voices,
Splashing like a whale?
The voices echo in the night,
The voices rumble in the day,
Oh! Have you heard the sea voices?

Fishermen have heard the sea voices,
Whispering, shimmering, splashing,
But they say it's just a tiny shoal of fish,
Whispering, shimmering, splashing,
But I know it's the *sea voices!*

Tom Campbell (9)
Henleaze Junior School

COBWEBS

Cobwebs are soft and tremendously silky,
Made in beautiful patterns,
So delicate, a touch of the cobweb, it breaks,
It's as soft as a feather,
Or maybe softer.

Serena Lenz (8)
Henleaze Junior School

My Mum Is Wonderful

M agnificent
Y ummy food she gives me

M ore work every week
U ntil she does it
M ust be hard

I t's not easy
S ingle mum

W onder woman
O n the go
N o one can stop her
D oes as best as she can
E veryone likes her
R ushing around
F arah is her name
U ntil she is fine
L ovely mum, she is the best.

Hope Gallie (11)
Henleaze Junior School

A Sleepy Puppy

Yawn, 'I'm sleepy' said the puppy,
'I'm as sleepy as a sloth.'
His tail was feebly wagging,
His face was slowly sagging,
He ran quickly to his basket . . .
And fell asleep upon it like a sleepy,
But still fast roadrunner!

Lauren Byrne (8)
Henleaze Junior School

DREAMER

I creep in, it's pitch-black,
The earth beneath my feet is moving.
I reach out for something to hold,
There's nothing there!
My world is disappearing.

I've clearly won,
I've won the lottery,
I'm cheering, the audience is clapping.

Dripping from a cloud is rain
And I'm on the cloud,
Floating gently in the sky.

I, I wake up . . .

Emily Thompson (9)
Henleaze Junior School

THE EAGLE

There's an eagle flying in the sky
In the mountains, flying high,
As golden as the sun, so high,
As elegant as the clouds passing by,
Claws as strong as diggers,
Eyes as bright as the moonlight
And as blue as bluebells.
He is as smooth as a sandy surface,
And that is why they call him
King of the birds.

Henry Moody (8)
Henleaze Junior School

JACK AND THE BEANSTALK

There once was a young boy called Jack
He was a hefty bully, as a matter of fact
He decided he wanted to make some cash
So he stole a cow and in a flash
He sold it for five small beans
An unreasonable deal, so it seems
He buried them under the ground
Where (he thought) they would not be found,
But when he woke up he gave a squawk
The beans had turned into a giant *beanstalk!*
Jack climbed it quickly, but had to stop -
A giant's castle was at the top
He looked inside and there sat
A kind, old ogre on a mat
Jack crept past him and stole
A hen, a harp and a bag of gold
The harp shouted, the giant gave a cry
Jack ran as if he was going to die!
He climbed down the beanstalk as quick as lightning
The giant was (after all) quite frightening
The giant pursued him, in his boots
He was unhappy with the awful brute
Jack found a sword and started to chop
(The ogre was still halfway up)
The giant fell with a deafening shout,
But where he landed he crushed that lout
That bully, that horrid, bulky terror,
But now Jack is flat forever.

Robbie White (11)
Henleaze Junior School

HUMPTY DUMPTY PARODY

Humpty Dumpty sat on a wall,
Smashed his head on a very hard ball,
His yolk fell out and he called for his friends,
Who couldn't put Humpty together again,
They used sticky stew
And they used super glue
And poor Humpty really needed the loo,
'You can't go to the loo my dear, dear friend
'Cause we can't stick you back together again.'
'Please try, please try my lovely old chums,
'Cause you're really hurting my podgy little tum.'
'I'm afraid we're going to have to leave you here.'
So they all went off and had a pint of beer.

Joseph Lovatt (10)
Henleaze Junior School

THE SCALE DRAGON POEM

Skin like
bumpy stones.
Feet like
penguins' flippers, all dull, soggy and wet.
Scales like
little exotic flies, flying around his body.
A head like
a massive pear,
all squishy.
Eyes like
fresh little grapes
and his body as hard as stone,
big and strong.

Danielle Yeomans (9)
Henleaze Junior School

DO I HAVE TO?

'Do I have to wash the dishes, Mum?
Why can't the cat?'
'I'm really sorry honey-bun,
He has to sit on his mat.'

'Do I have to clean my room, Dad?
Why can't the dog?'
'I'm really very sorry lad,
He's sleeping like a log!'

'Do I have to finish my work, Mr?
Why can't Sue?'
'I'm afraid Master Blister,
It's really up to you!'

Rebecca Steven (8)
Henleaze Junior School

TORNADO

A tornado is:
As dominant as a lion;
As muscular as a rhinoceros;
As omnipotent as the Queen;
As overwhelming as a whale;
As invincible as a Tyrannosaurus rex;
As consuming as a tidal wave;
As forceful as an explosion;
As deadly as a poisonous gas;
As overpowering as the sun.

Jamie Hughes (10)
Henleaze Junior School

THE BLACK-HOODED MAN

If you look out the window in the
Middle of the night

There's a black-hooded man who
Gives me a fright

He climbed into my bed
One night

I gave him a cold stare and he
Returned it with a glare

He glared to extreme so I let
Out a scream

Then I woke up and it was only
A dream.

Finan Rodinson (7)
Henleaze Junior School

DINO IN THE DEEP

Down in the deep
Where the dinos sleep
And the snakes slither and slide

Down in the deep
Where the whales weep
And the snakes slither and slide

Down in the deep
Where the frogs leap
And the snakes slither and slide.

Becky Hughes (10)
Henleaze Junior School

BLACK CAT

The inky cat prowls softly across the ground,
His sleek, black coat making no sound,
Eyes glistening emerald green,
He's midnight black, cannot be seen,
The moon is full in the star-stained sky,
As the mysterious cat slinks magically by,
He's elegant and silky, he struts and he preens,
Midnight black, he can't be seen.

Emma Watson (11)
Henleaze Junior School

THE SHARK

It swims so slowly around the sea,
Hiding to catch its prey,
It won't give up, it is very desperate,
It just waits around all day,
It will eat anything that it sees,
That's its favourite thing to do,
To do that all day, never bores him,
He'll even try to eat you.

Carla Ahmadi (11)
Henleaze Junior School

PINGU, THE KING OF PENGUINS

Pingu, the king of penguins
Stood majestic, tall and proud,
With jet-black eyes,
That sparkle like stars
And red top hat firmly placed.

He takes his bow slowly,
As his suit tails sweep the rink,
Scattering splinters of ice
Up to glitter and dance,
In the cool, dazzling moonlight.

Emily Adcock (11)
Henleaze Junior School

WHAT'S THAT?

What's that rattling on the draining board?
What's that climbing up a tree?
What's that moving on the window?
It surely can't be me?
What's that rattling the pencils?
What's that swimming in the sea?
What's that hiding in the gutter?
I'm sure it wasn't me.

Nicholas Adams (8)
Henleaze Junior School

GREECE

Greece is as hot as a boiling oven,
There are lizards slivering on the ground
And there are wet and wonderful seas,
The sand is soft when you have bare feet.
There are turtles floating in the sea,
It is a wet and wonderful place,
For me, I would rather stay
In Greece than Bristol.

Stephanie Melarickas (8)
Henleaze Junior School

I Remember, I Remember

I remember, I remember,
My first day at school,
I was very nervous,
But not afraid at all.

I remember, I remember,
My first friend I met
Was Julia Andrews
And she had a pet.

I remember, I remember,
No I can't, yes I can,
I can remember!

Hattie Haynes (9)
Henleaze Junior School

My Cat

I've got a cat called Jeremy
I think it is not fair
Mum gives him all the treats
And acts like I'm thin air.

Mum plays with him all the time
And why not me?
She lets him do all the things
Like climbing up a tree.

All I want her to do . . .
Why can't she just see . . . ?
Can't she just see
All I want her to do is pay attention to *me!*

Louie Newlands (8)
Henleaze Junior School

PIRATES

Oo arr, fire the cannons.
Oo arr, scrub the decks.
Come on, get out of your hammocks,
You lazy, slacking wrecks.

Up the Jolly Rodger,
Down your other boats.
We sometimes raid the farmland,
But only get the oats.

If you're not in a pirate crew,
Come and join the gang!
You get to drink both wine and beer
And you talk awfully slang!

Stefan Pollitt (9)
Henleaze Junior School

SPORTS DAY

Sports day lasts till the sun goes in,
But I don't like it much, I can never win.
Other people say it's good and fun,
But I like it when it's over and done.
For I've had three years at sports day
And never won.
Something always goes wrong,
My hat falls off or my shoelace is undone.
I go home with no prize at all,
I met the girl who had won the skipping race,
I had tried that but was too tall!

Emma White (9)
Henleaze Junior School

THE DREADED GUM

'Mum, there's gum stuck on my shoe,
It's sticking really well like glue.'
'Well, how did you get it on there?'
'What happened was that I didn't take care.'

'Mum, I tried to pull off the gum,
And now it's stuck to my fingers, so help me, Mum.'
My mum by now was getting mad
And said that I was a silly lad.

I took off my shoe and grabbed a pair
Of pliers that were on the stairs.
I tugged and tugged at the gum,
'Hooray, it's off!' I yelled to Mum.

Nicola Rees (10)
Henleaze Junior School

TINY TIGER

He swaggered through the jungle,
Feared by the other creatures,
Inclined to ensnare his prey,
He stalks into his lair,
Alert and attentive.

His jungle is the lush, green grass,
His prey he does not eat,
But tosses it from paw to paw
And his lair is the squalid garden shed.

Well it's not easy being a tiger
When you're a kitten!

Hazel Stenner (10)
Henleaze Junior School

I'M SCARED OF MONSTERS

I'm scared of monsters,
They could be lurking anywhere.
Even at the bottom of the stair,
They could be lurking anywhere.
They could be lurking in my bed,
Waiting when I get in.

Max Molton (7)
Henleaze Junior School

RIVER

Rushing, rushing, rushing,
Trickle, trickle, trickle,
Rapids, rapids, rapids,
Smooth, smooth, smooth,
Stop!
We've hit a rock,
Flow over the top,
Down the mountain,
Quickly flow,
Can't wait to get to the sea,
Beckoning fish to come our way,
Beckoning to come with me,
Can't find my way through curved pathway,
We've hit the rapids,
We'll cascade down,
Nothing will stop me now,
There's plenty of people with plenty of thirst,
I must get to them in time,
I'm through the worst,
I think I'll burst and let all the tiny fish go!

Rachel Drew (10)
St Mary's CE Primary School

HIDDEN TREASURES

I have hidden treasures
Many of them found,
I have hidden treasures
They are all around.

I have hidden treasures
They're only mine to keep,
I have hidden treasures
Some in my heart so deep.

I have hidden treasures
I keep them close to me,
I have hidden treasures
Some in my heart so deep.

I have hidden treasures
I like them oh so much,
I have hidden treasures
Like a friend and such.

I have hidden treasures
With them I'm happy to be,
I have hidden treasures
They're so important to me.

I have hidden treasures
I think of them in bed
I have hidden treasures
They're up there in my head.

David Poole (9)
St Mary's CE Primary School

SWIMMING IN A RIVER

I'm swimming through a river,
with all the fish I shiver.

To the bank I want to get,
look at that fish I just met.

It has rainbow-coloured skin
and flaps and swishes its fin.

I've got to where I want to be,
it's a wonderful place to see.

Now it's time to go,
I start in the river very low.

I'm swimming through a river,
with all the fish I shiver.

Amber Crookes (10)
St Mary's CE Primary School

TREVOR

His eyes are like diamonds
His skin is as soft as silk
His knuckles are as bumpy as mountains
His hair is as spiky as needles
His legs are as hairy as a sheep
His teeth are as white as the moon
His arms are as soft as warm fur
His heart is made of gold
Trevor is my brother.

Jennifer Jones (9)
St Mary's CE Primary School

WATER

Send me rushing down a stream,
Where I may have already been,
By getting recycled
From one tiny water droplet,
Through a tap, down a drain,
In a bath tub
I have been.

Send me down a waterfall,
That I have already seen,
By being used again and again,
Over the world, in the ocean,
I have definitely seen.

But the best thing of all is
I can float in the sky
And it takes me a long, long, long
Time to die.

Sheryl Thompson (10)
St Mary's CE Primary School

MY DOG, ARCHIE

My dog's fur is as black as coal,
His claws are like sharp daggers,
His tongue is as rough as sandpaper,
His eyes are like black marbles,
His paws are like small, not ripe apricots,
His tail is sometimes as curly as a snail's shell,
His nose is like a wet, black stone,
That's my dog, Archie.

Rebecca Williams (9)
St Mary's CE Primary School

MY CAT

My cat has big, brown eyes
like stars shining brightly.
My cat has great, white teeth,
they are so bright they look like the moon.
My cat has a long black and brown tail,
like a long snake.
My cat is quite shy,
like a small, little hamster.
My cat is as warm as toast.
My cat's fur is very long,
so that if she has any fleas they will get lost in it.
My cat is my best friend.
My cat is the best thing that ever happened to me.

Stephanie Thayer (9)
St Mary's CE Primary School

RIVER POEM

Water running down the river
Splishing, splashing
Launching into the rocks
Splishing, splashing
Flooding everywhere
Splishing, splashing
Current keeps on coming
Deep and shallow
Splishing, splashing
Quick and shallow
Splishing, splashing
Gentle and rough.

Richard Organ (10)
St Mary's CE Primary School

AROUND THE WORLD

Where would you go if you could go anywhere?
Taj Mahal, the Pyramids or sat home in a chair?
Thousands of places in the world to see,
From Western to Venice to Liberty.
I travel off to Paris, in France,
Where they stay up till midnight and dance.
Next to New York in America,
They have a different accent all the way over there.
Say hello to Italy and the Leaning Tower of Pisa,
They make pasta and ice cream and even pizza.
To China we go, to see the Great Wall,
Then over the sea to Niagara Falls.
Back home to England, to Bristol, to Yate,
I think I'll always remember this date,
As the day I travelled around the world
And the seven wonders were unfurled.

Heather Nicholls (10)
St Mary's CE Primary School

MY MUM'S HANDBAG

In my mum's handbag there are pens and paper, old books too,
There's probably a cuckoo clock, cuckoo, cuckoo, cuckoo.

There're credit cards and old receipts,
There're apples and grapes that she's got to eat!

There're Chocolate Buttons, Smarties too,
There're also old party invites, I wonder to who?

Jenna Youell (9)
St Mary's CE Primary School

RIVER

Out of a spring I come tumbling
A fish with a wish to reach the sea
Into a river, a stronger flow
Wandering gently as I go
Sparkling, quivering, two ducks on a bend
Surely a life as a fish has no end
Eventually the river reaches a town
Swimming strongly, never to drown
Under a bridge, a wave overhead
All the other fish easily lead
To a hook with a piece of bread on the end
I crave for the sea just around the bend
In the sea finally I'm free, a fish with a wish to be in the sea.

Rachael Ware (10)
St Mary's CE Primary School

MY FRIEND, RYAN

His hair is like a very thin, black, furry mat,
His eyes are like eggs but not very big,
His mouth doesn't move much,
But when it does, it doesn't stop for a while!
He also helps when I'm stuck
And gets me out of tricky situations,
His arms are like thin bits of rubber, all soft and squidgy,
His legs are muscly like a tyre,
I can also tell when he is sad by the look in his eyes
And I can trust him.

Josh Gouge (9)
St Mary's CE Primary School

MY CAT, BUFFY

My cat's eyes are like an owl's
And her fur is like a dark room,
Her claws are like daggers,
Her tail is like a black snake,
The cat's ears are like a tent
And her whiskers are like grass,
She is fast as a lion
And she is the best pet ever.

Matthew Thomas (9)
St Mary's CE Primary School

MY HIDDEN TREASURE

My hidden treasure is bright and colourful,
My hidden treasure is warm and cuddly,
My hidden treasure is beautiful, he is running free,
My hidden treasure is small and short,
My hidden treasure gets in trouble a lot,
It's my . . . puppy.

Mark Pearce (11)
St Mary's CE Primary School

HIDDEN TREASURE

My hidden treasure lays asleep in my head
While I lie and think and lay on my bed
Swaying waves and seagulls as well, fearing winds they are swell
These things are what I fear not
I don't know why but these thoughts won't stop.

Ben Heath (11)
St Mary's CE Primary School

MY BEST FRIEND, JOSH

Josh helps me when I'm stuck on work,
He has brown hair that is very short,
Josh is tall like a very short lamp post,
His hands are hard like rocks,
I can see when he is in trouble by the look in his eyes,
Sometimes he tells me secrets,
I can trust him when I'm sad.

Ryan Morgan (9)
St Mary's CE Primary School

MY HAMSTER

My hamster was my best friend,
He cheered me up when I felt down.
He had little beady eyes
And a tiny nose.
His back legs were covered in fur.
My hamster was small, cute and angelic,
I miss him and loved him lots.

Jade Chisholm (9)
St Mary's CE Primary School

MY FISH

My fish has skin like pure gold
He can swim as fast as a motorbike
He loves me with all his heart
He goes up like a speeding bullet
And he loves me and my family too.

Daniel Norris (9)
St Mary's CE Primary School

HIDDEN TREASURE

Is your treasure a sealed thought?
Something your friends could never have bought?

Can it be heard by a human ear?
Is it something which brings a cheer?

A treasure only you can see?
A faraway place or a cup of tea?

A holiday where you have been?
A place of glory only you have seen?

A slow-paced river, it could be?
A place on your own, so you can be free?

I have a secret hidden treasure . . .

Oliver Slade (11)
St Mary's CE Primary School

RIVER

Outside my house is a river
When I step in the river I shiver
Me and my friend
Have fun with no end
On the bank of the river

Outside my house is a river
I stick my hands in and the ripples quiver
Me and my mum
Have so much fun
On the bank of the river.

Laura Cropley (10)
St Mary's CE Primary School

HIDDEN TREASURE

A sparkling trinket box,
Bursting with fun and laughter.
Who goes there?
A mysterious hand
Dips in and grasps the gold.
One-too-many silver rings
Are captured without thought.
A box without meaning
Is a sparkling trinket box.

A sparkling trinket box,
Oozing with dull and gloom.
What goes there?
A soaring, murky cloud
Dips in and steals all thought.
All love and cherish
Are swallowed away mischievously.
A box without meaning
Is a sparkling trinket box.

No one knows what will happen
In my sparkling trinket box.

Sophie Youell (11)
St Mary's CE Primary School

THE RIVER

R is for rain, that fills up the river
I is for ice, when the river freezes
V is for valleys, where the river flows
E is for emerald, the colour of the water
R is for rapids, where the water is rough.

Paul Timms (10)
St Mary's CE Primary School

HIDDEN TREASURES

Have you found your hidden treasure?
I have not, but it would be a satisfactory pleasure,
A treasure could mean all sorts of things,
It could even be something that nature brings,
Exquisite flowers, newborn lambs,
Even an old tree, that's magnificently grand!
A treasure could, somehow, be a hobby,
Someone's could be golf or even hockey!
A chest of money? It could be -
Which pirates hid, possibly up a palm tree?
Now I remember my desire -
To sit with my family beside an open fire!

Timothy Higgs (11)
St Mary's CE Primary School

JAMES

James likes being naughty,
He likes girls,
He likes his scooter,
He wants to be a car painter,
He likes getting dirty,
He's fast at running,
James likes playing football,
He likes gel pens,
He likes trainers,
That's my best friend, James.

Antony Jowett (9)
St Mary's CE Primary School

THE RIVER FLOW

There's a current flow
that goes quick and slow.
Wet and dry, shallow and deep,
wherever you are.
Sand, mud, gravel, stone, rock,
down the loch into the lake.

Down, down, down, the waterfall goes,
even though it's a small flow.
Steep and gentle, flat and vast,
the worst thing is, will it always last?
Such a pretty sight, can't stop watching
and at the bottom, eggs are hatching.

Lauren Carr (10)
St Mary's CE Primary School

HIDDEN TREASURES

There are many hidden treasures
Some could even be pleasures
You can find them in the sand
Or somewhere not on land
They could be in a drawer
Or maybe on the floor
But most hidden treasures
You treasure and keep
Where no one can get to them
Or take a little peep.

Michael Radomski (11)
St Mary's CE Primary School

HIDDEN TREASURES

I get to my feet,
Dive into the water,
I swim down on further,
It seems to get darker.
I see loads of fish,
Something shiny ahead,
Should I go forward
Or back instead?
I carry on swimming,
To where it is led,
A small, golden coin,
In a seaweed bed.
I pick the coin up
And take it home safely,
I put it beside
A photo of my family.

Harry Drysdale-Groves (11)
St Mary's CE Primary School

HIDDEN TREASURES

Treasure hiding
Divers diving
Waves lapping
Fish flapping
As they get deeper
Their steps become steeper
Then they see a golden chest
They open it 'for the best'
They've found the treasure
That had been lost forever!

Amie Chinn (11)
St Mary's CE Primary School

HIDDEN TREASURE

I'm the hidden treasure
it has got to be me
of all the competitions
more than litres in the sea

People say I'm sporty
that life is up to me
come on you can pick me
I'll be the best that can be

Then about my friends
they are special to me,
but there isn't as much love
as in my *family!*

Lauren Saunders (11)
St Mary's CE Primary School

HIDDEN LAND

She is just a fairy,
Dancing in the air,
Her hair is so curly
And so fair.

There's a shimmering pond,
Which is near,
If only I could find it,
It would take away tears.

There's a diamond at the bottom,
It's so deep,
Is this really real
Or am I just asleep?

Francesca Kelly (9)
St Mary's CE Primary School

DARK, DARK HOUSE

In a dark, dark alley, in a dark, dark house,
Down the dark, dark stairs lived a secret treasure
Of dreams that come to life.
Every day a new hidden treasure
Pops down the dark, dark alley, down the dark, dark house.
Down the dark, dark stairs into the secret treasure box.
Every month a dream comes out of the treasure box
And up the dark, dark stairs, out of the dark, dark house,
Back down the dark, dark alley into the bright, bright daylight
Where everything comes to life.
Things like dead mummies singing and dancing.
Bad things come to the daylight and do stuff like
Rip people's insides out and gobble them up
'Til they're full up completely.

Ryan Brockwell (11)
St Mary's CE Primary School

HIDDEN TREASURE

I'm feeling lonely now that you've arrived,
I wish I was back in dream world.
Where the flowers smelt like honey
And the wind danced with the leaves.
Where the birds sang sweet songs
And the water trickled through the pebbles
And the fairies pranced around.
The people were so very light-hearted,
But still they were lost in their own little world.
My head is full of things to say,
But now all is lost since you've come to stay.

Elizabeth Seery (11)
St Mary's CE Primary School

HIDDEN TREASURES

All those simple hidden things,
Would stop us all from being kings.
A king can banish you from towns,
Those simple things take away frowns.
And sitting on those massive thrones,
Taking money from your loans.
To stop us all from being rich,
Changing white to a greyer pitch,
From all those things to queens and kings,
Give it up for all those little things.
From a blanket to a little cloth,
Or to just a little broth.
To be a king with all those pleasures,
I'd give it up for hidden treasures.

Laurence Murray (10)
St Mary's CE Primary School

HIDDEN TREASURE

I have a hidden treasure, hidden in my mind
A hidden treasure, that nobody can find
It's calling me all day
Please get me out some way
If only I could stop it saying
'It's only me you are betraying'
This is giving me a fright
Is this happening in the night?
Yes, it was a dream - my treasure
It will go on forever . . . and ever.

Verity Olivia Thorne (11)
St Mary's CE Primary School

HIDDEN TREASURES

Deep, deep under the sea,
Atlantis lies beneath me.

Gold, diamonds and riches,
Merpeople swim in dishes.

They swim so beautifully
And reach for the gold.

They are covered in jewels,
Each one sparkling.

I've gone down there,
But they don't care,
. . . it's hidden treasures.

Sophie Youlden (10)
St Mary's CE Primary School

BARNEY

Barney is as brown as mud,
He's got eyes like dark fir trees,
He's got black flint claws,
Whiskers like wires,
Ears like floppy triangles,
A nose like wet leather,
He's got a paw shape in the middle of his eyes,
He's got teeth like shark fins,
He's got legs like horses' legs
And elbows like soft mountains,
His tail is like a scruffy rope,
Barney is the best dog I've ever met.

Amy Greaves (9)
St Mary's CE Primary School

HIDDEN TREASURES

On a misty, mysterious night,
When the moon is shining bright,
My little treasure glows,
My little treasure sparkles,
When it is safe.

When the trees wave in the dark
And it glistens in the park,
My little treasure shimmers,
My little treasure shines,
When it is quiet.

My little treasure glows,
My little treasure sparkles,
My little treasure shimmers,
My little treasure shines,
Because it is a secret crystal.

Chloë Daniels (10)
St Mary's CE Primary School

HIDDEN TREASURE

My hidden treasure is far away,
I dream of it all night and day.
It might be a mystery land,
With calming sea and golden sand.

I'm sure my treasure is lost forever,
I wish I could float away like a feather.
I know one day I'll find my treasure
And live on an island with a lot of pleasure.

Claire Stirling (10)
St Mary's CE Primary School

PENGUINS ARE SO COOL

Lovely, cute, black birds
Graceful swimmers in the sea;
Love to play all day and night
Even before their tea!

White tummies, orange beaks,
Very friendly too!
They are my hidden treasure
And there are more than two!

They have wings and they can fly,
Only in the sea!
Their home is where it's cold
The one place I wouldn't be!

Marcus Skinner (11)
St Mary's CE Primary School

HIDDEN TREASURES

Silver and gold all inside
the big brown box,
good thing I lied.
When I'm older I'll be rich
and have super powers like a witch.
I'll buy a golden convertible car
and have my very own bar.
I walk nearer to the secret box
and find a golden diamond lock.
A silver key is underneath,
wrapped inside a crispy leaf.
I pick it up and poke it in
and all that's in there, is a book.

Katie Lansdowne (11)
St Mary's CE Primary School

HIDDEN TREASURES

Hidden treasures in coats and pockets
Hidden treasures in golden lockets
Hidden treasures in cupboards and drawers
Hidden treasures like dinosaurs' claws
Hidden treasures like thoughts in your mind
Hidden treasures that we lose and find
Hidden treasures like songs and prayers
Hidden treasures like grizzly bears
Hidden treasures we treasure and love
Hidden treasures like cream white doves
Hidden treasures like chewing gum and sweets
Hidden treasures like chocolate treats
Hidden treasures like strawberry ice cream
Hidden treasures like fairytale dreams
Hidden treasures in winter trees
Hidden treasures like the summer breeze
Hidden treasures we love to keep.

Laura Prickett (11)
St Mary's CE Primary School

SECRET LOVE

My love is like a bright red candle,
It flickers in my heart,
Oh how your eyes shine so bright,
Like two clear diamonds in the night,
Your voice makes my heart go bang,
Just like the song you sang,
Because I just love you in my heart.

David Pearman (10)
St Mary's CE Primary School

MY ANNOYING FRIEND

'Can I work with you?'
'Yes.'
'Can I sit next to you for lunch?'
'Yes.'
'Can I play with you?'
'Yes.'
'Can I come home with you?'
'Yes.'
'Can I go in your house?'
'Yes.'
'Can I sleep?'
'Yes.'
'Can we stay up?'
'*Yes.*'
'Can we watch TV?'
'*No, please go home!*'

Josh Matthews (9)
St Mary's CE Primary School

MY HORSE

My horse is pure, satin black,
His eyes are like the night,
He would not harm a flea,
He's so soft and warm,
He runs as fast as lightning,
My horse talks to me and understands me in every way,
My horse has a hoof which is like his mum's,
His teeth are like rocks,
My horse has legs which are very, very strong.

Jade Flynn (9)
St Mary's CE Primary School

MATCH OF THE DAY

Kit on,
Boots clean,
Sing a song,
Pitch green,
Start match,
Mat catch,
Yate scored,
St Nic's bored,
Sun shone,
Kit on,
Boots clean,
Sing a song,
Pitch green,
Start match,
Mat catch,
Yate scored,
St Nic's bored,
Sun shone,
Yate won!

Liam John (9)
St Mary's CE Primary School

MY BROTHER

My brother has a long, thin head,
His eyes are blue like the sea.
My brother's mouth is like a horse
And he shouts like thunder.
My brother has feet like Big Foot,
His hands are like his feet.
My brother has skin like a baby's bottom,
His hair is black and long, *yuck!*

Hope Winton (9)
St Mary's CE Primary School

CHARLOTTE

Her head is like a football,
Her hair is like the inside of a tree,
Her eyes are made of sky,
Her teeth are like sweetcorn painted white,
Her hands are like grannies'
Her legs are like stones in her skin,
Her nails are like square plastic,
Her skin is like soft paper.

Emily McKane (9)
St Mary's CE Primary School

HIDDEN TREASURE

My hidden treasures
Are bracelets and things
All gold and silver
Precious to me
Also my photos of family that's gone
My most secret, secret treasure of all
Is my friends and family that will be here for all.

Toni York (11)
St Mary's CE Primary School

MY HIDDEN TREASURES

My hidden treasures are my mates
My hidden treasures are my dates
My hidden treasures are my pets
My hidden treasures are my debts
My hidden treasures are my teachers

My hidden treasures are my preachers
My hidden treasures are my bears
My hidden treasures are my cares
My hidden treasures are my fears
My hidden treasures are my tears.

Hazel Kirkham (11)
St Mary's CE Primary School

HIDDEN TREASURE

My hidden treasure is pirate booty,
To find the treasure is my duty.
It's hidden somewhere, I don't know,
In the dark they will glow.
If I find it, I'll be rich,
Won't be living with a witch.
If I have lots of money, change,
I'll have my own shooting range.

Jim Pittaway (11)
St Mary's CE Primary School

HIDDEN TREASURES

Down, down, down in the secret ship
Lies a deep, deep, deep treasure chest
And in that treasure chest lies something secret
And that something secret, something gold
Something rare, something incredible
I know what it is
Treasure!

Liam Robert John (10)
St Mary's CE Primary School

MISS POWELL

Miss Powell is my teacher,
She teaches in class 5.
Miss Powell is my teacher,
She is the English teacher.
Miss Powell is my teacher,
She teaches the netball team.
Miss Powell is my teacher,
She has a fish tank in her class.
Miss Powell is my teacher,
She's got brown hair.
Miss Powell is my teacher,
She has to wear glasses.
Miss Powell is my teacher,
She is the best.

James Faulkner (9)
St Mary's CE Primary School

MY FAVOURITE CAT!

He moves like a graceful swan on water,
He has emerald-green eyes,
His ears look like silk,
His nose is shiny and soft,
He has bright white teeth,
He has the smoothest fur,
He has white paws made of satin,
He has claws that look like candy,
He has a long, swishy tail,
He is my favourite cat,
His name is Falstdaff.

Rachel Pellow (9)
St Mary's CE Primary School

PATCH, MY GUINEA PIG

His eyes are made of minute black stones,
His fur is made of smooth grass
Painted black, brown and white.
His little legs, so pink and rough,
His snuffly nose, so wet against
My cheek when I stroke him.
His spiky whiskers, pure white,
His teeth are as sharp and as shiny as knives.
That's Patch and I love him!

Bethany Gent
St Mary's CE Primary School

NIBBLES

My chinchilla, Nibbles is as white as snow,
He has little pink ears, red eyes like beads,
His back feet are like rabbits' with tiny claws,
His front teeth hold the nuts and raisins when he eats them,
He has a coat as soft as silk,
He is the best pet I have ever had.

Charlotte Hall (9)
St Mary's CE Primary School

UNDER THE BED

Under the bed monsters sleep
Under the bed eyes peep
Under the bed people dare not look
Because under the bed people can be took.

Sophie Blackmore (9)
St Mary's CE Primary School

ALONE IN A GARDEN

Alone in a garden except for the things I smell,
Sniffing the red, yellow and pink roses
And the scent of the grass just been cut.

Alone in a garden except for the things I hear,
Picking up the bees buzzing,
The tune of the birds singing sweetly
And the birds flapping their wings silently.

Alone in a garden except for the things I touch,
The wind brushing past me,
The roses feels like velvet
And the grass felt like crystals under my feet.

Alone in a garden except for the things I see,
Behold the red, yellow and pink roses,
The birds soaring through the air
And note the bees buzzing around me.

Danielle Sealy (9)
St Teresa's School

THE BEST TREASURE OF ALL

Up onto the shipwrecked boat
We set ashore while afloat
To a forbidden land which does hold
The finest treasure that man's been told
So you've been warned
About the greatest pleasure
Of silver and gold
That man could hold.

Bridie O'Neill (10)
St Teresa's School

ALONE IN A GARDEN

Alone in a garden except for the things I see,
Eyeing the beautiful red and blue flowers
And seeing the birds fly, twist and swoop from the sky.

Alone in a garden except for the things I hear,
Listening to the birds sing
And hearing the wind whistle and the bushes rattle.

Alone in a garden except for the things I touch,
Stroking the soft, silky petals of the bluebells and roses
And smoothing the fresh grass and leaves.

Alone in a garden except for the things I smell,
Sniffing the fresh grass and beautiful flowers
And smelling the fresh air.

Luke Bowler (9)
St Teresa's School

ALONE IN A GARDEN

Alone in a garden except for the things I see,
And those crows looking back at me,
I look at the flowers watching out for itching powder
Although I can't see,
Berries, are they poison
Or are they good for me?
Looking up at that big high tree
What a challenge it would be.

Alone in a garden except for the things I touch,
And the cat touching me,
I can feel the soft petals on my fingertips
And the bushes on my skin.

Patrick Maxwell (9)
St Teresa's School

ALONE IN A GARDEN

Alone in a garden except for the things I see . . .
The viewing of the flowers caught my eye.
The spotting in my eye of a little robin redbreast.
I was looking at a bunch of roses
And the sighting of the birds bathing and feeding their babies.

Alone in a garden except for the things I hear . . .
Listening to the lovely birds singing in the sky
I was overhearing the creaking of the door shutting after me *'creak'*
And I picked up the birds wings flapping in the light blue sky.

Alone in a garden except for the things I touch . . .
The extremely soft petals on the roses
And I felt the breezy air on my face
I stroked the soft leaves on a small tree.

Alone in a garden except for the things I smell . . .
The lilacs and I were sniffing the smells all around the garden
And they were very nice
And also the colours were lovely
It made me feel relaxed and warm
With a very little breeze on my face.

Caroline Voke (9)
St Teresa's School

ALONE IN A GARDEN

Alone in a garden except for the things I see.
Looking at a tropical parrot sitting in the tree.
I also see flowers red as can be.

Alone in a garden except for the things I smell.
Sniffing perfume coming from the flowers.
I also smell the freshness of the air.

Alone in a garden except for the things I hear.
Hearing the wind rustling through the tree.
Also hear the river rushing through the stream.

Alone in a garden except for the things I touch.
I smooth a deer as dear as can be.
Also touch a unicorn but it shuffled at me.

Maisie Milton-Newland (9)
St Teresa's School

ALONE IN A GARDEN

Alone in a garden except for the things I see,
Examining the flowers planted in the soil
I turn my head to a different sight
Where a pond is laying by a shed
The splashing of fish making water fly by
A movement in the trees where fruit grows
A water fountain where the water explodes into the air
The sights I see make my hair stand on end.

Alone in the garden except for the things I hear,
Listening to the song of birds
I pick up the sound of owls hooting
Hearing the eerie sounds of rustling in the bushes
Although the sounds I hear make me tremble.

Alone in the garden except for the things I smell,
Sniffing the scent of flowers
Different kinds of pollen inside
The smell of raspberries and strawberries
And other fruits
Alone in a garden except for the things I see, hear and smell.

Ross Jones (9)
St Teresa's School

ALONE IN A GARDEN

Alone in a garden except for the things I see,
Looking at a bird tweeting to me
I also see a big bunch of red roses across a lovely green garden
I must have dreamed them.

Alone in a garden except for the things I smell,
Sniffing a shiny sunflower like the smell of perfume
I also smell the lovely fresh air
Blowing around me to the lovely ground.

Alone in a garden except for the things I hear,
I hear the wind as calm as can be
I also hear a fateful sneer of runny water near my ear.

Alone in a garden except for the things I feel,
I feel a spiky tree like a hedgehog
I also feel a bunch of hay
I say, I say, I say.

Toni Stadon (9)
St Teresa's School

HIDDEN TREASURES

Treasure glints in the sand
No one even takes a glance,
But when a little child comes by
They fall into a trance
They grab their little spades and dig
As hard as ever can be,
But all they find under that
Is the glistening, blue sea.

Hannah Williams (11)
St Teresa's School

ALONE IN A GARDEN

Alone in a garden except for the things I see,
Looking upon a tall tree with blossom all around
Staring at bright red berries glistening in the moonlight.

Alone in a garden except for the things I hear,
Listening to an owl hooting in the dark
Hearing the leaves rustling in the wind.

Alone in a garden except for the things I smell,
Breathing in the aroma of flowers sweet as perfume
Sniffing up the freshly-mown grass.

Alone in a garden except for the things I feel,
Touching the cool night air on my face
Smooth the rough tree bark
Feeling the soft dirt under my feet.

Ben Summers (9)
St Teresa's School

ALONE IN A GARDEN

Alone in a garden except for the things I see,
Looking at a row of roses
And they are like a sweet.

Alone in a garden except for the things I hear,
Listening to the birds singing a song
And the song was good.

Alone in a garden except for the things I touch,
Feeling a dog like it had been playing in the grass.

Alone in a garden except for the things I smell,
Sniffing a rabbit it smells like it had a bug in there.

Ryan Cron (9)
St Teresa's School

ALONE IN A GARDEN

Alone in a garden except for the things I see,
Bright red roses as red as blood
And overgrown plants as tall as a beanstalk
And a tree as bare as an empty corner
And leaves blowing through the air
Like an aeroplane soaring across the sky
And daffodils as bright as a fresh banana.

Alone in a garden except for the things I hear,
Like birds whistling and the wind blowing
Like it's never blown before
And I hear the grass crunching beneath my feet.

Alone in a garden except for the things I touch,
Like the wind blowing through my ears
And the rocky floor beneath my feet
And flowers as soft as silk.

Alone in a garden except for the things I smell,
Roses as sweet as sugar
And the smell of weeds
Which makes you want to sneeze.

Julia Fox (9)
St Teresa's School

ALONE IN A GARDEN

Alone in a garden except for the things I see,
Noticing all the petals of a rose which is like a cherry
And observing the lovely neat grass which is green as a pea.

Alone in a garden except for things I touch,
Stroking all the lovely pieces of bark which is as rough as sandpaper
And embracing all the leaves of a tree, rubbing it against my face.

Alone in a garden except for the things I hear,
Picking up the things that fill my eardrums such as . . .
The cuckooing of birds and the smooth, soft sound of the wind.

Alone in the garden except for the things I smell,
Sniffing all the things like the scent of a lily
And breathing in the nice fresh air and blowing it out again.

Joseph Fitzgerald (9)
St Teresa's School

ALONE IN A GARDEN

Alone in a garden except for the things I see,
Looking at the scenery, how lovely could it be,
Everywhere around me different plants to admire,
Different shapes and sizes, and colours as beautiful as a rainbow,
The singing of the birds high up in a tree,
Sun shining down on me, I wonder if it can see?

Glancing at the roses pink, red and white,
Roots spreading underground and flowers starting to sprout,
I wonder if this is okay to feel and to smell
No one can see me, so I might as well.

Alone in a garden except for the things I touch,
Feeling all different kinds,
It's a bit much.

Soft and spongy, round and curved,
So many different colours,
I feel buds and bushes, fully grown flowers and even thorns,
This must be a dream or so it seems,
Wishing I would be able to feel it again,
In my own garden.

Jade Clark (9)
St Teresa's School

ALONE IN A GARDEN

Alone in the garden except for the things I see like . . .
Roses as red as blood,
Buttercups as yellow as the sun,
Bluebells as blue as the sea,
Fruits of all shapes and sizes
And nuts you thought you'd never find.

Alone in the garden except for things I hear like . . .
A falling of a nut, a rustle in the bushes,
A stone roll into a pond,
I hear the wind's soothing noise.

Alone in the garden except for the things I touch like . . .
The petals of a flower,
The bark of a tree,
The cold, cold ponds,
The roughness of a conker shell
And a soft lily pad.

Joshua Williams (9)
St Teresa's School

ALONE IN A GARDEN

Alone in a garden except for the things I see,
A hedgehog scurrying under the grass
I hear birds singing
Touch a lovely flower
Smell a lovely flower
Rising from the soil.

Reece Wynne (9)
St Teresa's School

ALONE IN A GARDEN

Alone in a garden except for the things I hear,
Shuffling from the crunching leaves by my feet
And the little hedgehog digging all the crunchy leaves out of its way.

Alone in a garden except for the things I see,
Red coloured roses that look like blood has been dropped on them
And all of the beautiful petals flying and spinning around off their stalk.

Alone in a garden except for the things I touch,
I stroked the beautiful petals that are the colours of the rainbow
And rubbed the soft grass below my feet
And the rough stone I feel next to my toes
And the flowers sway across me like velvet.

Alone in a garden except for the things I smell,
The scent of those flowers is beautiful
It was like the best perfume in the world
And the beautiful smell of wildlife.

Rebecca Slater (9)
St Teresa's School

FAMOUS TREASURE

There is such a thing as treasure,
on the mountainside,
over the hills and far away,
it just caught my eye.

Many, many animals stay with the treasure,
some people say that on that day
it was there forever.

Jordan Vailes (11)
St Teresa's School

ALONE IN A GARDEN

Alone in a garden except for the things I see,
Staring at a rose as red as blood
Staring at birds singing a lovely tune
Staring at the trees blowing in the wind
The wind blowing everything in sight.

Alone in a garden except for the things I hear,
Hearing birds sing a tuneful song
I hear the wind going shh, shh, shh
I hear a rabbit nibbling at leaves.

Alone in a garden except for the things I touch,
I touch a petal, it waves away
I touch a thorn, it pricked me
I touch a rabbit cute as can be
I touch a pond, it gleams, sparkling
It was wet.

Ryan Jones (9)
St Teresa's School

ALONE IN A GARDEN

Alone in a garden except for the things I see,
Looking at the leaves of a beautiful tree.
Staring at the sky all misty with clouds
And sighting all the flowers that I see now.

Alone in a garden except for the things I hear,
Listening to the wind all crystal and clear.
Hearing the crunching of my feet as I walk along
And overhearing the birds as they go singing songs.

Alone in the garden except for the things I touch,
Feeling the petals of roses as such.
Clutching some flowers to bring to my mum
And stroking my back in the heat of the sun.

Alone in a garden except for the things I smell,
Smelling a fence that smelt like Hell.
Breathing in the air that's all around me
And sniffing the scent of the flowers I see.

Quang Nguyen (8)
St Teresa's School

ALONE IN A GARDEN

Alone in a garden except for the things I see,
Looking down at me is a cute, little birdy
That's tweeting at me
I also see flowers that are round as can be.

Alone in a garden except for the things I hear,
I hear the sound of the wind that's blowing down at me.

Alone in a garden except for the things I touch,
I feel the lovely blossom tree
And I feel the lovely red rose that's pouting at me
And I feel the rabbits that run round me.

Alone in a garden except for the things that I smell,
I smell the lovely blossom that's on the blossom tree
And all the red roses that smell so nice.

Nathan Leaver (9)
St Teresa's School

ALONE IN A GARDEN

Alone in a garden except for the things I see
Like the flowers, the red ones were as red as blood
And the others were just like Haribo
I could hear a dog next door
But I took no notice of it.

Alone in a garden except for the things I hear
Like people are in the garden with me but there's not
And I can hear some birds in the trees.

Alone in a garden except for the things I touch
Like the smooth leaves and leaves below my feet *crunch.*

Alone in a garden except for the things I smell
Like hay from next door and the flowers.

Stephen Dillon (9)
St Teresa's School

WET, WET RAIN

The rain feels cold
as it falls on my hand
it gently pitter-patters
as it falls on dry land.
As rain comes upon me
I won't get a tan
I think I'll stay drier
if I wait in the van.

Madeleine Gould (11)
Stockwood Green Primary School

RAINY TREASURE

Wet and wet, more every day
I always wanted to go out and play
Rain, rain, rain, I hate the rain
Sun, sun, sun, I like the sun
Run, run, run, I like to run
Why, why, why does it
Always rain?
I wish to be always
In the shiny sun.

Yat Man Chan & Charlotte Gallop (8)
Stockwood Green Primary School

RAINDROPS

It sounds like bird feet.
Sometimes it's like sleet.
Pitter-patter on the rooftops.
When the raindrops land they suddenly go pop!

Lucy Seager & Emma Bowen (8)
Stockwood Green Primary School

TREASURE IN THE RAIN

Pitter-patter, fast as a rat that comes last in a race
Drops like thunder
Sounds like a wonder
Dropping on the silver roof.

Casey Beardmore
Stockwood Green Primary School

THE BEACH

Sun
Sandy
Bucket
Spade
Donkey
Water
Sea
Salt
Ice cream
Swimming costume
Trunks
Ride
Wave
Pier
People
Towels
Sun tan cream
Lollies
Itches
Gold.

Alice & Donna
Stockwood Green Primary School

ABOUT: CUSTARD AND MUSTARD:

I love custard on top of mustard
It makes my eyes go watery green,
But my mum normally screams!

Custard with mustard makes my eyes go green
I normally have bad dreams,
Then she covers my pudding with ice cream!

Vicky Lovell (9)
Summerhill Junior School

NANNY

We played merrily and she hugged me,
Now she's gone.
I think, with a look of concentration on my face,
It's very weird.
I won't ever forget pretending we were pop stars!

She was always peaceful even when she was cross,
Lying in another world.
Pleasurable memories flood my brain, thinking, crying,
She has disappeared.
I gave her flowers to show my affection.

My trustworthy Nanny, faithful, honest,
But fate came . . .
Her unbuttoned cardie smelt of love.
Gone.

Martha Ellie Dennett (9)
Summerhill Junior School

BIKE CRAZY

I am bike crazy,
Round and round, really mazy.
In and out, loopety loop,
Up and down, coopety coop.
I love my bike it is red,
And my seat is really comfy, like my bed.
There are all sorts of bumps,
Also a lot of jumps.
I like going up the big rock ramps,
I feel like a champ.

Alice Pople (9)
Summerhill Junior School

I Wish I Was A Bird

I wish I was a bird
Flying fast and free
Across the oceans and the sea
Around the cliffs and mountains
Not like you and me
Wings are bright and beautiful
Feathers soft and sleek
Little beaks singing all through the summer heat
Soaring, gliding through the sky
Watching, waiting, hearing every noise
Birds that shelter in the trees
Are small and weak in the breeze
Birds have wings of gold
That shimmer and shine in the bright sun
I wish I was a bird
Flying fast and free.

Lucy Anning (9)
Summerhill Junior School

The Sea

The sea is a pearl, twisting and shimmering bright.
The sea is a diamond, which has just been polished and shined.
It is a blue star twirling, and being washed down to Earth.

The sea is blue Fairy Liquid, which takes your breath away.
It is a blue sticker, stuck on the most glorious jumper.
The sea is a blue clock, which was swishing and swaying around.

And the most *glorious,*
Shiniest pearl the sea washes upon.

Kerrii May Knighton (9)
Summerhill Junior School

THE THANK YOU LETTER

Dear Aunt Hilda,
Thank you for my underwear,
It is a bit big but I can grow into them,
It is a bit colourful don't you think?

Dear Aunt Hilda,
Thank you for the underwear,
Don't forget I'm a girl not a boy,
I don't like writing letters.

Dear Aunt Hilda,
Thank you for the underwear
I really hated them,
I don't want the same next Christmas,
I want something good.

Dear Aunt Hilda,
Thank you for the underwear,
They were for boys not for girls,
I really hated them!

Nikita Patel (9)
Summerhill Junior School

DRAGON

Dragon, Dragon breathing fire!
Eating people all the time!
Beware, they could strike at any time.

Get the army in position
Or you'll be in an unhappy position.

Lee Wilkins (9)
Summerhill Junior School

Cats

Cats are fluffy
and also puffy,
they miaow
but we don't know how.

They've got fluffy ears
and they have no fears,
dogs don't like cats,
but cats like pats.

They are colourful all the time
and I don't think they like mime,
they have got wet noses
and they smell like roses.

Ouch! Their claws are sharp
also they might eat a carp,
their short legs
are bigger than pegs.

All you can hear is their purr
I like to stroke their fur,
they like to jump,
in front of the fire they like to slump.

They've got a curling tail
they always love you, they never fail,
they have coloured fur,
it sounds nice when they purr.

Cats don't like people stroking their tails
and most cats are black, mostly they're males,
they're cute when they're small
and they might get lost in the mall.

I like the small, white cats
and they like to sleep on mats.
Cats! Cats! Cats!
I love cats.

Ellys Dickenson (9)
Summerhill Junior School

THE SPIDERS

It's dark! What can I see?
Something soot-black as small as a bee!
Crawling rapidly towards me,
That's what I can see.

How did the spider get in?
It may have scuttled out of the bin.
Or sprang out of a tin.
That's what I'm wondering.

How shall I get rid of it?
I may touch it if I sit!
I could spit at it
Or maybe slaughter it bit by bit.

What shall I do?
I need to go to the loo!
In comes Dad to the rescue.
Uh oh! Here comes another two.

Ashanti Walker (10)
Summerhill Junior School

MY HAMSTER SUNNY

My hamster Sunny
Runs around his cage,
He spends hours in his well.
He's a large, plump hamster
He loves to play.

He might run up your trousers and back down.
He'll climb on your shoulder
He will play with your hair,
He runs around in his ball.
He'll go in his tube,
He'll eat some food
Have a drink,
Then go to sleep.

Jessica Roberts (9)
Summerhill Junior School

MY FRIEND

My friend is a girl,
Who wears diamond pearls,
Her name is Betsey Wetsey,
Who loves eating spaghetti,
She can't climb a tree,
And she loves honeybees.

My friend is Betsey Wetsey,
Who needs her hair cut,
She hates all squirrel nuts,
She hangs around with me at school,
She likes to squeeze her oranges,
So someone take her off my hands please!

Hannah Whittaker (9)
Summerhill Junior School

SPOOKY NIGHT

Spooky night, spooky night
I am so scared.
Spooky night, spooky night
The books are all torn.

Spooky night, spooky night
It is pitch-black.
Spooky night, spooky night
The monsters hide in the sack.

Spooky night, spooky night
My bed is so safe.
Spooky night, spooky night
The monster's got bad taste.

Spooky night, spooky night
Hide under the covers.
Spooky night, spooky night
'But go to bed!' said my mother.

Nicole Dicker (9)
Summerhill Junior School

MEDIEVAL JOUSTING

Knights and courtiers enter the arena
Timbo, the jester, cheers
A bloody battle with axe and shield
Ends up with horse and spears

The battle is won by a brave knight,
But all is not revealed
For all that the knight has to remember it by
Is the clashing of sword and shield.

Hannah Richardson (10)
Summerhill Junior School

HIDDEN TREASURE

A man who worked on a pier,
Came all the way over to here,
He knocked on the door,
And stamped on the floor,
And went to get a carrier.

He fell in love,
One Friday night,
Then stepped on a dove,
Which gave a great fright.

They went for a meal,
And climbed a great hill,
He showed a lot of pleasure,
When he had found his treasure,
Which had been hidden nearly forever.

Katie Morton (11)
Summerhill Junior School

THE KID

He's left out there just on his own,
No talking to anyone that he knows.
There while his classmates are all poking,
What? Me with friends? You must be joking.
In they go from playtime at last,
But the kid? No, he's late for class.
With schoolwork he is just the same,
But other people are ready to complain.
Home time now, what a relief,
Getting ready for bed and brushing his teeth.

Mason Bowers (10)
Summerhill Junior School

MY PET, DUSTY

My pet, Dusty the guinea pig
Had hair like a fluffy, grey wig.
He ate orange carrot with a crunch
And always ate celery with a munch.

In the summer days he would look at me jolly.
Also he would look at me and think good golly!
His eyes were always glistening with gleam,
He would see us playing in his dream.

But now he has passed away.
We can't have lots of fun and play.
But I will send him a best wishes letter
To see if, in Heaven, he is getting on better.

Jennifer Pretlove (10)
Summerhill Junior School

IN SPAIN

I didn't want to come to Spain
But now I'm really glad I came
It's sunny and bright
But cold in the night

I don't want to go in the sea
Because it's nearly time for tea
The sea is cool
But I want to be in the pool

The air is warm and breezy
The pollen made my nose sneezy
On Tuesday we went on the water slide
On Wednesday we went on loads of rides.

Emily Church (10)
Summerhill Junior School

MY HAMSTER HAMMY

My hamster Hammy
Sometimes is confusing,
Because I may call
Her Sammy, if she's in her house.

Hammy likes her nuts
She stores them in her cheeks,
Then she'll go into her house
And stay there for weeks.

When she's walking into her tube
She looks really small,
But when she comes out of her tube
She really is quite *tall*.

Keagan Robinson (10)
Summerhill Junior School

TEDDY BEAR

T   eddys are fun to play with
E   ating and drinking with friends and teddys
D   o you like playing with teddys?
D   id you have a name for it?
Y   ou and me love teddy bears

B   e there for your teddy
E   veryone likes toys
A   nd teddy bears are the best
R   eady teddy? Let's go to bed.

Caitlin O'Shea (10)
Summerhill Junior School

SUNNY DAYS

On a hot, sunny day,
All you want to do is play.
If you're hungry buy an ice cream,
Or sit back and have a nice dream.
Let the kids play in the sea,
Don't worry about tea.
Have fun in the sand,
And I'll give you a helping hand.
Throw a beach ball,
But there's a hole, don't fall!
Have you got your sun hat?
Do you want a chat?
But now the day's over,
I'll hope to see you tomorrow.

Samantha Cox (10)
Summerhill Junior School

THE MOUNTAIN HIKE

I hiked up a tiring mountain
Wishing to see the top
A blizzard came
It swept my friends away
They did not survive
Desperate to get to the top
I carried on
Snow was trying to stop me
At this time I thought I would not make it
After many hours I made it to the top
What a treasure -
I survived!

Jack Jarrett (11)
Summerhill Junior School

My Family

My family is big,
My family is small,
My family is wide, short and tall.

My sister is annoying, she bugs me all the time.
She's too much of herself,
She thinks she's just fine.

My brother, well he's just a todd,
I bet when he grows up he'll be a little odd.

My dad can be quite funny and always makes a joke,
Wonder if he'll ever grow up?

My mum is always up and down the stairs,
Making beds and cleaning clothes,
She gets quite fed up as it goes.

As time goes by
I wish they'd be as normal as I.

Georgia Mead (10)
Summerhill Junior School

Dread

An hallucination drifts through the eerie twilight of the deserted lobby
And who can tell what it's seeking for
The reverberation of stampeding gales
It can't be a ghost you reassure yourself
As you glimpse through the counterpane
But the wilderness outside is hushed and restrained
And suddenly you are filled with dread.

Rosie Gauge (10)
Summerhill Junior School

Hidden Treasure

H ide-and-seek
I n and out the sea
D eep diving
D ancing in the water
E veryone's screaming
N ow we run

T ake a trip in a boat
R un till you sweat
E at all the food around
A nd find jewels in the sand
S et up a picnic
U se it so you can start a collection
R un to the bus
E veryone's back at the bus.

Paige Nethercott (10)
Summerhill Junior School

Happiness

H aving a sister is so great
A nd having a brother who's a mate
P uts a smile on my face
P laying with them in a race
I n the morning they will say
N o more nap time, it's time to play
E very time I say yes they say
S o come on then, get dressed
S o that's the rhyme of happiness.

Rochelle Sheppard (10)
Summerhill Junior School

SPRINGTIME

Spring is here! Spring is here!
It's a wonderful day,
Flowers are growing,
Children are spinning round and round,
The weather's all sticky,
Webs are hanging high and low,
The weather's so hot I need some more water.
Animals being born in different countries,
Birds are flying over to their homeland,
People walking around town, in and out of shops,
Barbecues start being held,
Parties go crazy,
Clubbers go mad
All different people get rid of their colds,
People go on holiday.
It's time for fun!

Jade James (10)
Summerhill Junior School

A NEW BABY BROTHER

A new baby brother will make me happy
As long as I don't have to change his dirty nappy
The presents that my family will bring for him
Will make me feel very dim
The attention that the will get
Will put my mum in full priced debt
A new baby brother
I hope will be never.

Ben Millard (10)
Summerhill Junior School

ME AND MY SCHOOL

My school and I are not meant to be,
We shouldn't be together, can't you see?
We never went together,
And we never will.

My name is Persistently Lonely,
I have never fitted in.
I am consistently alone,
I'm forever on my own.

I am always sat behind a book,
While others have a good look at me,
I'm really bad at football,
Because I'm really pygmy.

I'm never gonna fit in here,
I will fade, fade, fade.
I sit there watching,
The clock invariably ticking my life away.

Molly Winstanley (10)
Summerhill Junior School

TREASURE

T eddy bears and family will always be close to me
R ealising what I needed to know
E verywhere I go they will always be with me
A nd when I'm upset they will be with me
S o I know they will always be with me
U (my parents) will be with me every step of the way
R ecognising me everywhere I go
E veryone in my family will stay in my heart.

Becky Player (10)
Summerhill Junior School

HIDDEN TREASURES

How to find them, I do not know,
Until I find family, I have to go.
Great people died fighting in the war,
When I find it will know a little more.
Great-uncle Tom and other people,
I will do it if I have to climb a steeple.

Then an aged box I found,
Dirty, like it was buried in the ground.
When it was open, I found a picture,
I looked at it as if it was a weird creature.
My great-uncle in 1945,
Now I know, I wish he was alive.

I have found my family,
My hidden treasure, finally.

Nicola Gillam (10)
Summerhill Junior School

HAPPINESS!

H aving fun all the time
A nniversaries, birthdays and weddings make me happy
P uts a smile on your face
P eople are always up for a race
I cing is my favourite sugar thing
N anny likes to sing
E ating cheeseburgers is great
S o now Tanya, Beth and Rochelle are my mates
S o now I can't be sad.

Roxy Lawrence (11)
Summerhill Junior School

HIDDEN TREASURES

H ide-and-seek
I n and out the sea
D ive under, up for a breath
D ancing on the sand
E njoy the day!
N ow we go swimming

T ake a trip on the speedboat!
R un till you sweat
E at until you get fat!
A nd find a photo of your nan
S hop till you drop!
U se it to remember her in your heart
R un till the sand is out of your toes
E veryone's back on the bus
S ee your nan in your mind.

Kimberley Campbell (11)
Summerhill Junior School

HIDDEN TREASURE

T reasure's really hard to find,
R ich people are not very kind,
E ast and west, south and north
A nd if it comes down to me,
S aw a genie just for me,
U ranus is his planet home,
R ound and round the Earth he roamed,
E nded up at my poor home, is it where it's meant to be?

Natalie Woods (11)
Summerhill Junior School

MY BEST FRIEND AND I

My best friend and I,
Like eating blackberry pie,
We play football,
The goals, two walls.

When I score,
My best friend roars,
When he scores,
I act like an open door.

My best friend and I,
Wish we could fly,
If it came true,
Then no one would do what they do.

When we grow old,
Our heads won't be bald,
We will be slow,
One day you know.

Bret Ryan Tizard (10)
Summerhill Junior School

HIDDEN TREASURE

She makes me happy,
She holds my hand
When I despair.
If I'm sad she helps me.
She's loving and caring,
She's there when I need her,
She's my best friend.
She's Lynette.

Mellisa Louise Szabunas (10)
The Tynings School

HIDDEN TREASURE

Long, long ago, up in the attic
It was there
A hollow, golden parrot,
And an old, brown bear.

I was excited, delighted, and cock-a-hoop,
Under the parrot's tail, there was green goop,
His beak was sharp, and like a loop,
My dad said it was a fluke.

The parrot's tail was made of leather,
The bear's toes were padded with leather,
The bear looked pretty weird,
Under his fur, like a gusty beard.

I rushed down the single stair,
With my parrot, and my bear,
I quickly dashed into my room,
And closed my curtains,
In the light of the moon.

I've kept them ever since.

Jack Andrews (10)
The Tynings School

HIDDEN TREASURE

At the end of the rainbow my treasure lies.
Waiting for my friends to help me climb.
We get a ladder to get us up,
We slide down the rainbow all together.
We get up and look for my golden pen
And my friend Ben
Just found it just then.

Reece Powell (9)
The Tynings School

HIDDEN TREASURE

Lying on my bed, bored
Thinking of my friends
Wondering what to do
Mum shouts up
'What are you doing?'
'Nothing.'

Pop!
In my head I thought
To go into the attic
I climbed up the ladder
I looked straight on
And what did I see?
A glittery, gold, finest, new,
Beautiful necklace
Hanging from the ceiling.

I reached up
To get the precious, true necklace
It was there shining in my hands.

Hannah Durnell (10)
The Tynings School

HIDDEN TREASURE

I looked out of my kitchen window,
There was a cross on the ground,
I went outside to see if it really was
A cross on the ground.

I went to get a shovel and a bucket,
So that I could dig it up,
Underneath the cross there was a key,
Beneath the key there was a small box.

In the box there was a golden, sparkly,
Glistening bangle,
I was so amazed and excited,
I found out it was a surprise
From my mum and dad.

Katie Shipp (10)
The Tynings School

HIDDEN TREASURE

I've lost my precious hidden treasure,
It's nowhere to be seen.
I've looked upstairs, I've looked downstairs,
It's nowhere to be seen.

She's pretty, special and very precious too,
She's my little, tiny doll and I love her very much.
She's golden, well-dressed and my only one if that,
She's my little, tiny doll and I love her very much.

It was a gift from yesterday,
It was my birthday.
She played with me,
It was my birthday.

And then I saw it,
Her little leg,
Sticking out from under my bed,
Her little leg.

I jumped with joy at the sight I saw,
It was my pretty China doll.
I picked her up and hugged her tight,
It was my pretty China doll!

Kate-Louise Fry (9)
The Tynings School

HIDDEN TREASURE

I had a lucky charm from my mum,
She said it used be her mum's,
She said. 'It is a very special one.'

'Can I see it?' My mum said, 'Yes.'
I held it in my hands,
It felt special to me,
There were silver and gold charms on it.

My gran passed it around the family,
I will wear it when I go out.
It's a very old charm, it looks like it's new.
It had a secret locket on it and inside there was a picture
Of my mum and gran.

I am going to pass it around the family
And will it last forever?

Emma Hazlett (9)
The Tynings School

HIDDEN TREASURE

A treasure is not the purest gold,
That's hidden beneath the sea.
A treasure is not the pearls and gems
That sparkle like a bright star.

A treasure is not crystals and diamonds,
That holds a great fortune,
It isn't even fragile china,
That must not be broken!

This treasure is much more pure,
Than either gold or silver,
This treasure is part of you,
This treasure is your friends.

Naomi Cassidy (10)
The Tynings School

HIDDEN TREASURE

There was once a boy called Joe,
Running through the forest,
Whisking through the trees,
He carried on!
Pant! Pant! Pant!

'Ahhhhh,' he tripped,
'Ouch,' he shouted,
He spotted a crimson ring,
With gold diamonds,
He carried on!
Pant! Pant! Pant!

The ring sparkled in the light,
He stopped with fright,
He heard a noise,
He carried on!
Pant! Pant! Pant!

He stopped again!
He saw a ring-shaped keyhole,
He put it in . . .
It disappeared!
Pant! Pant! Pant!

Alex Seymour (10)
The Tynings School

HIDDEN TREASURE

Up in the attic a treasure map lay,
I only found it yesterday,
It was old and tatty,
The ink was smudged,
I could only just see what it was.

I started to follow,
It was really quite fun,
But here's the first obstacle,
A pair of roller skates on the top stair.

I dodged the skates,
But! Only just,
What - another hazard?
This time it's the dog,
Snorting like a hog.

I crept past, quieter than a mouse,
And now the back door,
I'm in the garden,
Where's the cross?
There it is.

I started digging,
Deeper still,
Until, there it is.
I pulled out the trunk and looked inside.
Oh no! It's a bone!

Sam Elliott (10)
The Tynings School

HIDDEN TREASURES

I'm sleeping in my bed right now,
Before I hear some rustling,
I look out the window, what can I see?
A turtle crawling around.

I jumped down the stairs,
And put on my coat,
And I skipped out the door
With a skipping rope.

It was golden and brown,
And had hair like a tidal wave,
So I named it Elvis,
Because it looked old.

I kept it a secret,
Before my brother knew,
He was ecstaticed,
And thought it was slimy.

And now my mother knows,
It comes out every night,
And sometimes gives my brother
A big, big fright.

Because the family knows him now,
And they like him very much,
They thought they could make him one of . . .

Us!

Ben Vincent (9)
The Tynings School

HIDDEN TREASURE

I have a best friend,
She's called Milly doll,
I play with her when I can,
And love her with all my soul.

One day, I woke up,
I couldn't find my precious friend,
I thought she was lost,
I was thinking it was all pretend.

I looked everywhere,
Even under my bed,
And there she was,
As still as the dead.

I ran downstairs,
And told my mum,
'I've found my doll,
Can I have a plum?'

Samantha Wood (9)
The Tynings School

HIDDEN TREASURE

I was playing in a field one day,
When I saw a huge cross
In-between the flowers,
I ran home to get my shovel,
I started to dig.

I saw a small, posh box,
When I opened it
There was a very delicate necklace inside,
It had a tiny dolphin on the end
Of the golden chain.

I tried it on,
It fitted perfectly,
I took it to the police,
But nobody claimed it,
The police let me keep it.

Faye Mason (10)
The Tynings School

HIDDEN TREASURE

Lying in bed
Thinking of my best friend
Wondering where she could be.

Reaching to my neck
Stretching to find my necklace
It's not there, it's gone.

My friendship has been broken,
I've lost my best friend's necklace,
I was devastated!

I ran downstairs to ask my mum
If she had seen my necklace.
'No,' she said, 'I only saw it on you yesterday.'

I searched and searched to my heart's content
There was only one place left to look,
That was under my bed.

Is it, it can't be,
Something glitzy in the sun,
My necklace, yes, I found it.

I was relieved to have it back,
I will always make sure it will never go missing again.

Connie Short (10)
The Tynings School

HIDDEN TREASURE

Under the archway of a rainbow lies
The twitters and tweets of the animals besides
And as the colours of the rainbow get darker
And deeper,
You can get happier than ever before.

Under the archway of a rainbow lies
The glistening green of the grass besides
And with the sun shining down onto
The roses below,
You can see just how they glitter and glow.

Under the archway of a rainbow lies
The hidden treasures of the country besides
And with the golden sun shining below,
I am lost with a wonderland glow.

Jade Morch (9)
The Tynings School

HIDDEN TREASURE

My mission is to get the shiny, gold treasure under the sea.
As I walk towards the sea,
I put my suit on and finally I dive down deeply.
I see the gold, I swim down deeper, I pick up the gold.
I see a speck of light as I swim up to the surface.
No one has seen me, I am very excited and run to sell the gold.
Thirty-two thousand pounds has come to me and my family.
We are all in joy, me and my family are finally rich.

Mission complete.

James Cox (10)
The Tynings School

Hidden Treasures

I have got a teddy bear
He is really old
He's always at the end of my bed
And sleeps with me at night

I adore him with all my might
And he adores me too
I got him in Disneyland, Paris
When I was about four.

I was thrilled when I got him
Because he is as sweet as ever
His name is Winnie the Pooh
Although he is dirty I still love him too

He is my treasure
All chubby and sweet
I love him best in the world
Because he is my teddy bear.

Rebecca Jones (10)
The Tynings School

Hidden Treasure

Nanny's clock makes me feel happy.
It ticks and tocks the time away.
Making me proud every day.
It chimes very sweetly when I am there.
And I think of my grampy as look at the clock.
As he z-z-zes and snores in his comfy chair.

Vicky Maggs (10)
The Tynings School

HIDDEN TREASURE

I have a locket,
That I'd like to keep in my pocket.

My mum said I would be a fool,
If I took it to school.

I keep it hidden in a wooden box,
Which is covered with a giant fox.

I was given it the day she died,
There's a picture of my gran inside.

It's a special treasure to me,
I will pass it on to my family.

Claudia Jacob (9)
The Tynings School

HIDDEN TREASURE

In the deep, deep sea,
Fishing with the nets.
Throwing the nest into the sea,
Pulling in the nets.
Pulling something heavy,
What could it be?
Asking his partner for some help,
Steadily pulling up the ropes
And to his surprise a chest appears.
Steadily pulling the chest on the boat,
Opening the chest, a stamp book inside.
A treasure to a boy.

Alex Gill (9)
The Tynings School

HIDDEN TREASURES

We are walking in the flatlands,
'Give me water,' George demands.
I stumble over a clump of heather,
Inside it is some hidden treasure!
Out I pull an ornate chest,
Reflecting the sun from the west.
And there before my eyes,
Rears a genie of great size.
'What is your greatest treasure?
Is it gold or is it leisure?'
But the biggest treasure I could see,
Was to have my grandad back with me.

Simon Tourigny (11)
Wrington CE Primary School

HIDDEN TREASURES

Once, under the sea
Lurked a treasure
Many people have gone for it
And never come back,
But I like swimming down and down
In the vast sea,
But there is a chest
I grab the handle
And pull up
Here it comes
When I get on land
I open it
There is shiny gold everywhere.

Simon Medd (10)
Wrington CE Primary School

MY BED

Sometimes I lie wide awake making up ferocious new creatures.
Sometimes I lie wide awake making up new games.
Sometimes I lie wide awake feeling quite hungry.
Sometimes I lie wide awake feeling quite thirsty.

I love my bed, I love my bed, it makes me feel at rest,
It's really snug and I love my bed, it's what I like the best!

It keeps me safe from any danger, bullying, my bossy sister,
At night I hug it and it seems to hug me too,
My bed holds me safe for ten hours,
And doesn't ask for thanks.

I love my bed, I love my bed, it makes me feet at rest,
It's really snug and I love my bed, it's what I like the best!

Sometimes I lie wide awake making shadows on the wall.
Sometimes I lie wide awake with today's memories running through
                                                            my head.
Sometimes I lie wide awake feeling quite lonely.
Sometimes I lie wide awake cuddling with my ted.

I love my bed, I love my bed, it makes me feel at rest,
It's really snug and I love my bed, it's what I like the best!

Mary Wratten (11)
Wrington CE Primary School

GWAIN'S ARMOUR

There once was a knight called Gwain,
Who was almost slain,
He cut up the green knight,
It gave his mother a fright,
And now he's left out in the rain.

Gwain owned some fine armour,
That he bought off a farmer,
It was worth a lot,
He's glad with what he's got,
And he rides on a llama.

Mathew Thorneywork (10)
Wrington CE Primary School

My Dog

My dog is black
My dog is lovely
My dog's name is George

My dog is sixteen years old
My dog is fun
My dog is messy

My dog barks sometimes
My dog is kind
My dog is good

My dog is like a person
My dog is healthy
My dog does what he's told

My dog is naughty sometimes
My dog goes for walks
My dog doesn't like fireworks

My dog likes food and water
My dog is noisy sometimes
My dog is caring.

Sophie Sleight (10)
Wrington CE Primary School

HIDDEN TREASURES

I go into the deep water,
I see shipwrecks covered in mortar,
I spy a treasure chest,
I think that I'm the best,
I bring it up to the top,
I then see a cop,
He thinks I've stolen it,
But I explain it bit by bit,
He then says sorry,
And sails off to Balacorni,
I finally open the chest,
And I see a golden bird's nest,
No, it's a crown,
Draped in a silk gown,
I go back to land,
I then place it on the sand,
Oh, what a great discovery!

Philippe Wilson (10)
Wrington CE Primary School

UNDERGROUND

Down underground,
Under our feet,
There are lots of creatures,
Fast asleep.

Spiky hedgehogs,
Nestle 'neath the trees,
Badgers burrow,
So far and so deep.

Moles dig low,
Rabbits make a hole,
If you see a tiny tunnel,
It might just hide a vole.

Amber Hartley-Watts (11)
Wrington CE Primary School

PARADISE

I swim through the sea
As happy as can be
With dolphins swimming by my side.

As I dive down steep
And meet creatures of the deep
And crabs that nibble my feet.

I swim to the side
And gaze up high
At the birds that fly in the sky.

I look up the beach
And stare at the trees
As the bees dance around their leaves.

I decide in my mind
It's time to find
A safe place to sleep for the night.

I find a place beneath the waves
In a beautiful crystal cave
I close the door and give the world one last wave.

At the end of the day
I lean back and say
'It's been the best day in paradise.'

Joanna Kim Marshall (11)
Wrington CE Primary School

HIDDEN TREASURES

It was hot and sunny on holiday, an exotic island far away.
I went for a walk along the beach,
To search some rock pools out of reach.
I came across a clump of rocks, surrounded by some sweaty socks!
That's the strangest to find, I thought out loud, in my mind.

Maybe a tramp dumped them there, or took them off to let them air.
I held my nose in case they smelled,
And through the package slowly delved.
Through the tiny rocks and socks, until I saw some shiny blocks.

I dug away and could not believe the sight I saw,
And I began to retrieve.
One, then two then three and more, small blocks of gold,
                                          shining galore.

Then I picked them in my sack, and quickly took a shortcut back.
Now I'm rich and have lots of bikes,
And always love my lonesome hikes!

Harvey Andrew Walters (10)
Wrington CE Primary School

TREASURES OF THE WORLD

In the murky waters deep,
Underneath a stone I peep,
There's a sparkle, there's a shine,
Look! A treasure, it's divine.

I have a toy, it is my treasure,
It gives me fun and hours of pleasure,
I cuddle it tight in my bed,
It snuggles up quite near my head.

The treasure of nature is lovely,
The sounds I hear, the things I see,
So much is there, more than I know,
All around us, some high, some low.

But the best treasure of all, anyone knows,
Is to be with your family wherever they go,
That's the treasure of love, it rules the rest,
It is the treasure that's definitely best.

Rebecca Millard (10)
Wrington CE Primary School

ALL IN MY BUCKET

At the bottom of my garden,
where nobody knows of,
I keep a bucket,
right underground.

In that bucket, I keep,
half the moon for the weather,
a golden heart for love,
and a photo of friendship.

I keep all my hard work
I have done at school,
my brother, my dad,
my mum and others

All in the same bucket.

Sophie Johnson (10)
Wrington CE Primary School

HIDDEN TREASURES

Down under the sea
Hidden by a wreck
Is anyone there?
You'd better check

Lots of creatures
Big or small
It doesn't matter
If it's tiny or tall

A crab in a shell
A fish swimming past
A slow turtle
A dolphin so fast

They swim through a wreck
Where pirates have been
It is a sight
That not many have seen.

Hope Cadman (10)
Wrington CE Primary School

HIDDEN TREASURES

Deep down I go to find a block of gold.
Then I saw a block, I thought it was gold.
But no, I can't find it anywhere.
I look here and there but I have no luck.
But then I saw a chest, it had a lock on it.
I saw the key by my foot.
I opened it up, and there it was,
A block of gold.

Matthew Beck (10)
Wrington CE Primary School

HIDDEN TREASURES

Under my bed where nobody goes
There's a box with all my treasures hidden inside
A piece of sky as blue as the calm sea on a tropical island
A ray of sunshine glittering and shimmering gold
The howling wind on a cold winter's night
Sparkling frost as cold as the midnight air
A slice of rainbow as bright as the brightest of suns
A flash of lightning soaring through the sky
A star from the darkest of nights
A fluffy cloud as light as air
The Man in the Moon with a big smile
The magic of a newborn butterfly woken from its sleep
A feather from a golden eagle up high nesting on a cliff
A unicorn hair as soft as a gentle breeze through the country.

Amy Frampton (11)
Wrington CE Primary School

WHEN I WENT TO FIND THE TREASURE

When I went to find the treasure under the sea
I saw a fish swim and a dolphin dive
When I went to find the treasure under the sea
I saw an octopus goggle at me and a starfish on the sand
When I went to find the treasure under the sea
I saw a crab crawl along the sand
When I went to find the treasure under the sea
I saw a shark swim past me
When I found the treasure under the sea
I heaved it to shore.
I never had to look for treasure again for I was
Rich!

Louise Basey (11)
Wrington CE Primary School

HIDDEN TREASURES

H ow I love the sea below,
I cecold as cold as snow.
D eep below the ocean's crown,
D eeper still, still deeper down.
E verything's so colourful and new,
N ow we can see it in the ocean blue.

T reasure of silver and gold,
R esting on the seabeds so cold.
E veryone is hoping to find,
A coin or maybe some jewellery of some kind.
S urrounded by shells, sea animals too,
U nder the coral they'll frighten you!
R ays of sunlight through the sea,
E ntangled seaweed around you and me.
S hhhh!

Hannah Shirt (10)
Wrington CE Primary School

HIDDEN TREASURE

In my bedroom I've got something,
It begins with the letter S.
They live on Mars in a tank,
It's treasure hidden from Mum and Dad.

The second word begins with M,
Have you got it yet?
You can watch them grow,
Feed them and see them hatch.

They begin as eggs,
And grow to adults,
But guaranteed to live two years.
The hidden treasure is Sea Monkeys on Mars!

Jennifer Vowles (11)
Wrington CE Primary School

FOOTBALL

Football is my life
I play it every week
I practise every day
Between the two white posts
Is where the ball
Needs to be

The green pitch
Your muddy boots
The crowd roaring in your ear
The ref's sharp whistle
When a bad challenge comes in

The excitement of a match
The desperation of a last goal
Before the final whistle goes

The sharp attackers
The swift defenders
The strong midfield
The acrobatic keeper
Keep this game alive.

Andrew Lund (11)
Wrington CE Primary School

THE MIND

The mind is a mysterious thing,
Some might even say it's a treasure,
A hidden treasure,
A treasure we take for granted,

And yet . . .
Where those who nurture and feed it,
Others kill and deface it,
They pollute themselves with drugs,
And fantasies of war.

The mind: so vast, yet so small,
More precious than gold,
Than silver and diamonds,
And yet, for some, it's wasting away.

James Harris (10)
Wrington CE Primary School

CORAL REEF

Down under the crystal clear water,
There's a bed of colours,
Where the fish roam and hide.

Go deeper and you will find,
Dolphins jumping up and down,
Fish are swimming around.

I go up for air and return to the harmony of the sea,
There's something there,
It's a turtle swimming happily.

A boat is coming,
It's a poacher looking for the turtle,
I hide behind a rock.

The turtle hides too,
The boat floats very slowly and passes by,
She was safe but for how long?

Emma Gilling (11)
Wrington CE Primary School

HIDDEN TREASURES

H idden treasures with me at home,
I love them so much,
D addy, mummy, sisters and brother,
D eep down there inside me,
E very day I think of them,
N othing would be the same without them.

T hey support me in everything I find hard,
R eading books when I was little,
E ating, sleeping and playing together,
A my 'my beloved' the name chosen for me,
S urprises at birthdays, Christmas and when I'm good,
U s all together, one big group,
R ealising that we should treasure each other,
E ntertainment brings laughter,
S o me and my family are full of hidden treasures,
  not the expensive kind.

Amy Vowles (11)
Wrington CE Primary School

HIDDEN TREASURES

I walked up the stairs to our old, smelly loft,
I opened the door and coughed and coughed!
Cobwebs were hanging, spiders were spinning,
I looked around but I could see nothing.

But then there in the corner I could see,
A treasure chest, as old and rusty as could be.
I slowly walked over and lifted the lid,
And there at the bottom was . . .

A bundle of letters,
A ring of gold,
A tear-shaped earring,
A postcard so old.

Lucy Evans (11)
Wrington CE Primary School

THE REEP

Down beneath the water lies
Hidden treasure buried deep
Local people say 'Lots of lies'
Someone diving too deep
Gets eaten by the Reep
One local boy he did try
In the Good Sub Butterfly
He dived deep
Even he
Did not see
The Reep
Too late!
So of the treasure beware
The Reep is waiting there!

Nicholas Higgs (10)
Wrington CE Primary School